THE ANIMALS' APPEAL

THE ANIMALS' APPEAL

Have Mercy!

Wind River

authorHOUSE®

AuthorHouse™
1663 Liberty Drive
Bloomington, IN 47403
www.authorhouse.com
Phone: 1-800-839-8640

First published by AuthorHouse   9/4/2009

ISBN: 978-1-4490-2703-2 (e)
ISBN: 978-1-4490-2600-4 (sc)

Printed in the United States of America
Bloomington, Indiana

This book is printed on acid-free paper.

WIND RIVER

Wind River has become a visionary writing artist, full of color, flavor and beauty. The Animals' Appeal HAVE MERCY is a fantasy adventure by the animals, for the animals and to the animals. We journey into the heart, mind, body and soul of the animal spirit.

A terrestrial traveling Dalmatian came waltzing into my life about the time I began my pioneering writing career. He became the dog whisperer, with a voice! He becomes the coachman, "the goodwill ambassador". On his own cosmic journey, in search of wholeness and virtue. The coachman meets the white soul bird and the traditional American Bald Eagle our dual stewardship, the icon Phoenix. THEY ROCK THE HOUSE!

Now let's fly for a minute on the wings "of gold" betwixt Heaven and Earth to the Seventh Heaven of the seven golden cockatiels, the color of the rainbow, who become victims of the three sisters of fate! Karma the Falcon, Mercy the Scarlet Macaw, and Grace the White Cockatoo. The vistas on the trail for the neglectfulness of the sacred temples, "SHAME ON YOU!"

The cockatiels transmute into the Iron Butterflies on the flip side of the Great Square Ladle and become saints of love hope and peace! in the Galaxy of Knodea where the Black Light Mustangs live and thrive, "The Mares of Deliverance." "I give thanks for the power of thought." -Wind River

CONTENTS

Free Winged Spirits...xiii

Bird of Thunder 1

The Big Bang! 5

Dodora's Precious Gems 7

Sacred Week.. 11

Creation Of Companion 23

(Emergency).. 25

Bakersville.. 31

Creation Of Companion 33

EMERGENCY at the Twilight Zone...HOLY MOLY!!!................ 35

Bakersville.. 37

Galaxy of Knodea.. 43

Banquet of Graces 61

ACKNOWLEDGMENT

I simply choose to be called Wind River, an ancient deity that guides her pen to enlightenment and enchantment. I'm a visionary; my turbulence will move your spirit and stir your imagination. It will stimulate your mind and warm your heart. My voice calls you to understanding in order to believe, to know, in order to accept and the virtue of wisdom in the treasured word. My wake up call, the poetic courtship of Morning Doves, Saluting, Gaea' The blue Beauty' My spirit rises thankful for the dawning of Aquarius the beginning of my song and dance. My time wise live long days, give way to the call of the majestic rulers of the night. "The Great Horned Owl" his realm; timed wisdoms, ancient knowledge and the totem pole of full moons and moon dogs. He charms the mid-night skies, with his majestic voice, the eve of Wind Rivers' flight and I can DREAM!

This spiritual quest will walk you in the foot steps of the brave, where there's no boundaries, no lines, no limits to the field of dreams, a spiritual ray-seekers' fantasy. The Animals' Appeal endeavor shall become a spiritual path of Wind River making. The birds and the beasts, the torch barriers of suffering and pain!

This fantasy novel is dedicated to the animals for the animals and by the animals. "Praise" To all the fine feathered friends, 'nobility' to beasts and Honor to man's best friend the dogs.

The first noble pet is Bell; she's our black beauty, a boarder collie, Blue Heeler, Bell, runs like Wind. Wind River was "Saved by the Bell". She's our Nobel Prize winner.

Our second honored pet is Liberty she's a black and white spotted, Labrador/Blue Heeler. She's my devotee, a dedicated companion and our obedience champion; my pride and joy! The two dogs coupled up as Liberty-Bell!

Next, I proudly present Romeo, a purebred Dalmatian; he came as a terrestrial wonderer, the scent of his master lost. His spirit guides carried him to the end of his trail; tail tucked. The still waters were calling his name, Romeo where art thou! His spirit was defeated; his body had run its last mile, weary and almost stone cold. The hands of the dog gods shined GRACE upon his face. His angels had arrived, "HAVE MERCY".

We restored his spirit, healed his body and brought back to life a magnificent beautiful beast. His spark of life came shining through, once the sparkle in his eyes returned. His spirit guides began speaking louder than words with his deep rolling rhythmic voice, singing praise. Saying; "Happy to be alive sister! Happy to be alive! Romeo has become a guiding light, and my inspiration. The voice in the Animals' Appeal a gift in return for a second chance. Wind River listened very closely as silence speaks; and seized the opportunity to write the words of wisdom through the voice that cries out of the wilderness. Our three dog are the physical reality which bring true life into the stories. Romeo is in our first book. Liberty the second book and Bell the third book. With the powers invested in Wind River; I proudly present to you "THE AMIMALS APPEAL HAVE MERCY"

FREE WINGED SPIRITS

Our free winged spirits, the Blue Birds of Thunder. These spiritual leaders will reflect in character, the mirrored images of virtue, personal talents, victories and defeats. Here's their low down;

The Phoenix and the American Bald Eagle; dual stewardship, the hermaphrodite. The thunderbird The four winds –the golden eagles

Alceto- the Falcon

Pied Piper the Turkey vultures

Mercy- The Red Scarlet Macaw

Grace- The Pink Cockatoo

The Morning doves-of peace and harmony's to serve with love

Dodora- Ameythest Cockatoo

Six cockatiels their cheeks the color of the rainbow the vistas

The Baker Brothers, Barn Owls

The Dalmatian- The Coachman

(K)-(9) - Two purebred Dalmatians

Juliet- A winged purebred Arabian a black light Mustang

Romeo– The Centaur, the horse-man Sagittarian

Mares of deliverance Team of purebred black light Mustangs

Diana-The white tail doe,

Two Moons-yin and yang white tail and black tail deer

Koomba-the unicorn

Father Time-The Great Horned Owl

Sand man the spotted owl

Mother Earth- "The Blue Beauty"

Atumra- the sacred cedar tree the gemstone guardian

Four golden eagles the four winds

BIRD OF THUNDER

The Egyptians occasionally represented the phoenix as having the body of a man and the wings of a bird. This biform creature had a tuft of feathers upon its head and its arms were upraised in prayer. As the phoenix was the symbol of regeneration, the tuft of feathers on the back of its head might well symbolize the activity of the penal gland, or the third eye, the occult function of which was apparently well understood by the ancient priest craft.

Both Herodotus and Pliny noted the general resemblance in shape between the Phoenix and the American Bald eagle, a point that the reader should carefully consider that the modern Masonic eagle was originally the phoenix.

DESCRIPTION; The body of the phoenix is as having been covered with glossy purple feathers while its long tail feathers were alternately blue and red. Its head was light in color and about its neck was a circlet of golden plumage. At the back of its head, the phoenix had a peculiar tuft of feathers, a fact quite evident, although most writers and symbolists have overlooked it.

The phoenix was regarded as sacred to the sun, and the length of its life (500 to 1000 years) was taken as a standard for measuring the motions of the heavenly bodies and also the cycle of time used in the Mysteries to designate the periods of existence. The diet of the bird was unknown. Some writers declare that it subsisted upon the atmosphere; others that it ate at rare intervals but never in the presence of man. The bird is described as using sprigs of acacia in the making of its nest.

The phoenix (which is the mythological Persian roc) is also the name of the Southern constellation, and therefore it has both an astronomical and astrological significance. In all probability, the phoenix was the swan of the Greeks, the eagle of the Romans, and the peacock of the Far East. To the ancients mystics the phoenix was the most appropriate symbol of the immortality of the human soul, the phoenix was reborn out of its own dead self seven times seven, so again and again the spiritual nature of man rises triumphant from his dead physical body. In the mysteries it was customary to refer to initiates as the PHOENIX or MAN WHO HAD BEEN BORN AGAIN, for just as physical birth gives man consciousness in the physical world, so the neophyte, after nine degrees in the womb of the mysteries, was born into a consciousness of the spiritual world. This is the mystery of imitation to which Christ referred when he said," Except a man be born again, he cannot see the kingdom of God" (John III 3) the phoenix is a fitting symbol of this spiritual birth.

Ovid tells the story of the Phoenix as follows: "most beings spring from other individuals; but there is a certain kind which reproduces it self. The Assyrians called it the Phoenix. It does not live on fruit or flowers, but on frankincense and odoriferous gums. When it has lived 500 hundred years, it builds itself a nest in the branches of an oak, or on the top of a palm tree. In it collects cinnamon, and spikenard, and myrrh, and of these materials builds a pile on which it deposits itself, and, dying, breathes out its last breath amidst odors. From the body of the parent bird a young Phoenix issues forth, destined to live as long as its predecessor did. When it has grown, it lifts its nest from the tree, its own cradle and its parent's sepulcher, and carries it to the city of Eliopoulos, in Egypt, and deposits it in the temple of the Sun." the Phoenix just before an era would disappear for a series of ages would revisit Egypt. It was attended in flight by a group of various birds, all attracted by the novelty, and gaze with wonder at so beautiful appearance. From the molding flesh a worm springs and when grown large, is transformed into the bird of thunder. Part of his plumage is golden and crimson. For the most part very much like the eagle in bulk and size.

The Phoenix is believed to have originated in the city of Heoiopolis

"That sole bird
When, to enshrine his relics in the sun's
Bright temple, to Egyptian Thebes he flies."
"So when the new-born Phoenix first is seen
Her feathered subjects all adore their queen,
In addition, while she makes her
progress thought the East,
From every grove her numerous train's increases;
Each poet of the air her glory sings,
And round him the pleased
audience claps their wings."
–Dryden.
(Hall 1977)

The American Bald eagle will soar with the master minds, as kindred spirits in light and flight of the ancient deity' the Phoenix" The Legend of Soul!" GET INTO THE SPIRIT! The Icons to the gateway to the ancient of days and the dreams of night. From the spiritual, to beyond the cosmos, to the soul birds of "let freedom ring" the rising of icons and oracles. The Phoenix, the thunder male, the eagle the bird, female, it will be a hermaphrodite we will call them Thunder Bird they will crawl, walk, fly, swim and sink! They will travel light, jump high, and stand tall. The Thunderbird in their combat for the right to life, in their vast world of cosmic wonder will move your spirit. Their virtues, the strength, their majestic power, their ancient wisdoms and knowledge may their light shine on you! From Foot prints in every sand to the Dog Star and beyond!

THE BIG BANG!

The sound vibration of all creation (AUM) began vibrating with the warm feelings of love. The heavens turned to sky blue swirling with the colors of indigo, the darkness of night and the light of day. The thunderbirds blue lighting struck the pentacles of existence. The blue thunder rolled, the vibrations alerted all the birds in the heavens, it was time for the first sweet melodies to begin, their kingdom come, their will be done between seventh heaven and beyond. They had been preparing eons for this moment.

Then all the masterminds of this creation clapped their wings from side to side, saying the nine sacred words. The four sacred winds appeared, bring their force, the breath of life, the blue lighting flashed, their golden colors twisted up into the zenith, shooting fireworks back down to the seventh heavens, turning all the heavens the colors of the rainbow the seven sacred colors of Earth to come "bod-a-bing" THE BIG BANG"! Mother Earth in her infancy was born and brings paradise to Seventh Heaven! The stars were set in motion.

All the heavens joined in singing praise to the master minds for the gift of free winged spirits. The angels, the white doves where created with their kindred loving kindness, they joined harmony's and became the opera divas singing praises to the new heavens, everlasting. The angels also took on the responsibility of being the overseers and spirit guides to all bird souls. When the infant is born into the sea of ignorance, angels are assigned to the birds, according to the stars under which they are born. The stars are fixed fates, the angels also are bound by the foundation set by the stars of inequity.

DODORA'S PRECIOUS GEMS

Dodora, the priestess, her temple was the highest honored of all the heavens the pyramid of pure nirvana and the eye of reason over all private and public affairs. This deity presides over the temples of the heart and souls of the Seventh Heavens, the sacred fires. Dodora's temple made of ivory, and the top capped with sapphire, the blue whale of pyramids. Thunderbird branded the sacred symbols of all things to come on to the steps of the pyramids and tattooed their bones with the sacred secret code, which will lead to the mysteries. Mother Earth, the chasm of all existence is a sacred soul to the Sun! He prepares a place for the journey to the cosmic Earth. The thunderbirds glory!

The holy fires are attended by the six virgin cockatiels and Dodora, the amethyst cockatoo. Their duties are to keep the sacred fires burning, never to let them burn out as the safety of the city was held together by these flames, and if neglected by the virgins, all would suffer the consequences.

The virgins' top Koch and cheek colors are the same as their soul mates' temples. They carried their colors elegantly with honor, showing their rank, being the only colorful virgins in all the heavens.

Dodora, mother of their immortal souls is the caregiver of their jeweled gems within and the guardian to the seven sacred flames. Four of the virgins hold the corner stone temples. In addition, Dodora, and her two favored daughters, Red and Orange, the youngest of the virgins guard the other two temples together. These being the seven major umbilical cords that when bound together will create the bodies of the beasts.

Dodora would go to the sacred grove with the others of her class. She was the torchbearer that would light the fires in the sacred groves. She would fill the grove with the essence of myrrh, frankincense and cedar wood incenses, soothing to their aged soul. Smoking their thought, as the colors fill the grove with the essences of the rainbow, sending colored smoke signals to the third eye, which leads to the ever expanses of the universal mind. The feelings of pure nirvana consume their soul's totality in spiritual Bliss when in this mind-set of their inner beings.

Dodora had a veiled side about her, in that she was never satisfied. After creating the virgin daughters, her womb became barren. Knowing that the joys of pregnancy sooths her inner cravings of a females womb. A comfort only a mare can know. At times, she would have feelings of jealous rage within her, the demon of the red dragon rises within her, her virgins were given the virtue of a quenched womb, being innocent and pure had no clue of the cravings living within.

Dodora assigned the virgins to each of her temples, to ensure that the fires would never reduce to the element of smoke, for the elders only. She instructed them to be attentive. "When I am away collecting and sending information about that which is to come, it will be your immortal souls at risk and mine if you let the temple fires reduce to the veiled smoke screens of ignorance! IT will be our eternal damnation, the atrocities of our free-winged spirits. DO-NOT-BE-Careless!"

SELFISH INTENT

Indifference within her character, preoccupied with her own self-pity…Instead of keeping to her temples she chose to satisfy her own inner longings with selfish indulgences, the cravings of lust for more, circumvent the void in her womb…A secret longing, knowing it was an undesirable trait in her position of royalty.

Red was bold enough to ask, "How could we possibly be condemned? We live in the abode of the Gods and we are immortal? (Which means in our realm, everlasting?) Dodora responds, "NEVER DOUBT THE HIGHER WISDOMS OF THE MASTERMINDS!"

SACRED WEEK

At this point in the heavens, the virgins were informed of the sacred week that was to come. The most sacred week in the history of the heavens (the creation of MOTHER EARTH). Dodora told them she was going to the celebration. She also knew that in a blink of an eye everything would be changed. Positions upgraded to a higher level of immortality.

She could not hold out, for the longings of her body consumed her reasoning. Her inner lusts, consumed her thoughts, it drove her back to the sacred grove, as a magnet to its counter part. All the other gods and goddesses had left the sacred groves for the last heavenly celebration as things were. She was indifferent to the feasting, singing and dancing of the heavens. She saw she was alone and thought she would take the prime opportunity to indulge one last blast from the past on her own behalf; self-gratification.

Alceto the falcon has a red tuft on the top of her head. Mercy the scarlet macaw has a blue tuft. Grace the pink cockatoo will become GRACE; these three spin the threads of destiny. They punish by their knowledge handed down to them by the keeper of records and the threads that bind! The MIND'S EYE of remembrance kept! Alceto being the eldest is the lord of vengeance and death; armed with razor sharp cutting shears, which can cut life short just to please herself.(Scout 1898)

Mercy is the deity of the doors which open both ways. With the pure in heart on one side and wickedness, which leads to death of the soul on the other? Then there is GRACE who is the deity which leads us to the pearly gates of those who are redeemed *Pure in Heart*!

Orange and Red could see the party of holy of holies was about to start, their mother was not watching and the party was luring. Red said to Orange, "Let's just get a little closer for a peak at the holy rolling party! It cannot harm any thing!" Red lightning struck, and the claws of fates scooped them up.

THE ALL SEEING EYES

They were snatched by Alceto's, to their everlasting damnation. As soon as the two were in her clutches, the warmth within became as cold as ice, emptiness filled their bones as their miserable mother. A falling feeling came over the virgins. A feeling they never experienced before. They were dropped into a big vat of dry ice, a freezing chill consumed them as the vat began teaming with the death comrades the stinking soul-eaters, a chilling environment!

Dodora flew to the sacred grove's exit the instant she hit the threshold she tumbled to the ground, head over heels, her wings had been cut. All was dark in the seventh heavens; she could feel a gravitational pull under her feet. She would stumble and fall as if the terrain was rocky and rough. She no longer had a guiding light. It was a very uneasy feeling accompanied by cold feet. She realized the three sisters of fate had taken her free roaming spirit... She had been deceived as she herself had defied all her comrades.

Dodora was exhausted from the weight of her feet. *Feet Suck!* she thought. (As she approached the temples, she could only see a mirage curtain vapor in the place if her once blue bonnet Temple.) A moment's glimpse and down came the claws of fate, carrying her off the think tank where her daughters were placed. The ice had risen to the top of the tank and her virgins were at the brink of drowning, a very uncomfortable feeling. Being pulled down like a magnet, bound by the threads that bind.

GRAND SLAM

Alceto ascended to the reaches of the outer limits with Dodora in her clutches. Her stomach had the queasy feeling of falling, yet she was being elevated upwards. To give her a glimpse of what could have been hers, beyond the zenith. Her eyes wide open, bulging like the Red planet pressures. Her atrocity she would never see clearly again. Smoke felled her eyes, it once was a pleasure, but now a tyrant. A dim outlook circumstance she had brought upon herself.

Alceto released her, and she pearl dived with every herding inch becoming heavier and heavier. The load on her shoulders grew with ignorance. Her veiled selfish indulgence had become her own deception.

Dodora came hurdling down like a ten ton whale. She slammed into the vat Kuboom it hurdled red and orange to the otter limits, they saw their life pass before them. Then their lights went out, as they pearl dived back to the dungeon floor, belly-up. The virgins were still holding their breath, until blue in the face, a very uneasy feeling. They hit the flood; it knocked the wind out of them.

These three tyrants spoiled the PERFECT PLAN! They held up the rest of creation it was put on hold until the Fates make up their minds!

With their virtues stripped, their stars and stripes pulled out from under them. The virgins had no protections left and would become vulnerable to the threats of Alceto and her ways! Alceto cut loose, a burning like heartburn filled their souls, and an unquenchable thirst and hunger consumed their bird bodies. The black storm clouds of violence, the turbulent twisters of sinister, and the roaring thunder of the red dragons. Where the light of love cannot live. In addition, darkness will follow them all the way to the depths of the seas of ignorance.

COLORED

Alceto cut loose with her cutthroats, she then flew back to the seventh heaven for the other four virgins. The four virgins **Yellow, Green, Sky Blue and Indigo** were the only four left in the seventh heaven. They wondered what was wrong with them. Virgin green ask her sisters do you think it was because we have **COLOR.**

At that moment a very cold gale force wind came swirling in with roaring thunder. They trembled with fear, Alceto, rattling their spirits a little. She said to them, YOU WILL BE MINE ONE

FINE DAY my little colored pretties with wicked laughter, she thinks, just a little mental javelin will do!

Once a very special goddess, but now you must pay the PIED PIPER, IN MY ABODE OF THE TORCHERED, and the realms of the dead! With a very wicked witches laugh, accompanied by a chilling cold that screamed into the core of the innocent four virgins. Feeling a cold chill. While in her clutches she would smear a little of her inherited wealth on them.

Alceto enjoying her few moments of sending her personal pleasures upon these young virgin goddesses. Because they were still innocent, pure and unknowing. They were almost petrified with fear, a feeling they had never experienced before ------------ Sky Blue says, "Heavens to Betsy, what have we done?"

HAVE MERCY! Mercy shouted, at that moment they were in Mercy's temple. Alceto backs off retreating to the higher powers. Mercy has compassion in her heart for those who choose to walk the path of light, with 100% faith and no doughty, from her aged wisdom. She invited **her** sisters, the fates, to be a part of the plan. The four innocent virgins knelt down before the sisters of fate, with their beaks on the floor of Mercy's temple. It had mystical scent of myrrh and cinnamon surrounding them, bringing peace to the mind, heart and souls.

The virgins, trying to express their true colors like peacocks fanning their tails. Using their gem powers still within to portray themselves as brilliantly as possible, bowing before their superiors.

FOURWINDS THE FOUR WIND SPIRIT DEITIES,

NAMED: **NORTH, SOUTH, EAST AND WEST. They were the solar sun deities of the Thunderbird, the granddaddy's of blue thunder and Light. They had been given the powers to bring the winds of change upon the heavens of the most** high...these four winds were the apples of his eye, the golden eagles, the North Wind brings the gongs, the East Wind brings the trumpet, the South Wind the whistle, and the West Wind a hoot. **SPECIAL AND SACRED.**

(BAD-HAIR-DAY)

You could hear them coming like a jets, speaking their motto. Once the four winds arrived at the Temple, they could see why they were being drawn like magnets to the scene, JUSTICES OF FATE! The virgins' fate waits! Looks like a bad hair day for the accused. These seven last issues stand in the way of the sisters of fate, and their free winged spirits. Condemned or set free was the question.

The virgins were commanded to hit the floor with no hesitation. The turbulence began; bolts of red lightning struck from Alceto, the roaring thunder of her red dragon appeared. She shouts CONDEMN, with turbulent terror, they have the blood of the red dragon in the veins, Visual aid! Grace shouts softly Have Mercy, Mercy says give them a chance. The four winds watch intently, the gong sounded the ringing of the ears began. They could only feel the heat and hear her roaring dragon. FEAR THIS! Nothing compared to it.

BLUE BLOOD

Indigo was the first, her noses bleeding blue, the first of the BLUE Bloods. Bleeding her inner light out, her Life as a goddess was dying, the end of her chapter. The remaining sisters could only hear, and feel a weakening coming over them as a part of their sister was dying in them too...

INDIGO'S feet curled as if too close to a fire. Her head began smoking and her feathers curled; then Poof she became a ball of fire, with the scent of burning feather. The other virgins listened with trembling fear. They could hear snapping and crackling and sizzling; they could feel the heat and smell the burning flesh and feathers. When the smoke cleared, her head was bald and her top conch had been stripped of its color. The first element in the house of fires. Alceto's purifiers. Indigo lay there with smoke still rising on her charred body. Her eyes plucked her mouth sealed shut. Indigos screaming was silenced as if in a bad dream trying to escape. All her virtues and talents had been stripped. The same fate awaits the others. Poor innocent virgins going through the wrath of the condemned. They were hysterical!

HAVE MERCY

HAVE MERCY! At that moment, MERCY intervened; she could see something was not quite right with Indigo. Her light was fading too fast.

Then Mercy requested Yellow, saying softly you are the daughter to the sun you will be pardoned, in due time, these words helped soothe her weary soul. Put your color around the necks of your sisters. Yellow tore off some of her silk scarf and felt her way to the others, saying "I love you, sis." Once she got to Indigo, she could feel that her body had been crispy-crittered, her sister moaning in agony. An elusion from Alceto. She began weeping for her own soul's fate and that of her sisters, as she ties the yellow ribbon from the old oak tree around their necks. INDIGO'S TEMPLE

There was a soft warmth that touched Sky BLUES back and a sweet scent that touched her soul. A breath of fresh air filled her lungs and a sigh of relief came over her. Mercy lifted Sky Blue up in her warm wings of Hope. Giving her a moment's rest, saying you will be OK. Mercy held her tight taking her back to Indigos temple, still smoldering. Sky Blue was left at the foot of the Indigos Temple. Pray hard for the soul of your sister while I go back to my temple.

ALCETO'S PLEASURES:

Leaving the three vulnerable to Alceto's pleasures, Mercy told Alceto: "They are still in my temple keep your claws off them until it is finished!" Alceto bows with wicked intent.

Alceto speaks with fire in her eyes, and a roaring in her voice that was ear-piercing, "Ahh my little pretties, your days are done and you're mine. You just wait and see what I have planned for you!" As wind and fire came squelching and screeching from her soul. Then, fire and brimstone came out from her core, as her red cutthroats vomited from her wicked soul.

Poof her red dragons appeared, by her side the tyrants of terror. The stagecoach, of fire breathing red dragons held the vat with Dodora and the other two sisters Orange and Red. It was a terrifying event and a chilling sight. Cutthroats by the thousands with their shape cutting shears, snapping and snipping at the victims. Alceto says to her cutthroats, "You have your way with them as; I have to skip out for a minute." Her teamsters knew what to do "Singing their motto" Kick them when they're down"!

Alceto let loose her cutthroats to slice the throats of the virgins, so that they would bleed a little faster. Ahhh! Very well done with pleasing pleaser in her wicked voice, then she sucked her team up with her Gail force winds and swallowed them back into her self. Then laughed with wicked pleasure leaving the virgins as they were, untouched by her hands.

HEAVEN'S INSURANCE PLAN

(SKY BLUE) Eyes were still sealed shut. The ringing in her ears had stopped she could hear Indigos, the voice of reason in her head, saying have faith sister, have faith! At that moment Mercy popped in, this will put the mark of faith into your souls. Good things come to those who wait. Heaven's insurance plan!

Heaven's insurance.

TRAIL OF TEARS

The (trail of tears began falling from the remaining virgins eyes. Streams of their color ran down their faces, and breasts, covering with their hearts with their color dripping it on to the floor. Bleeding heart, EMOTIONS-run high, the raw open pain of injustice, the agony of the unsettled soul.

The virgin Yellow bled the most, her eyes having the liquid gold of the seed soul, the color that merges with all. Her tears were the river of life and the keeper of the soul temple. Yellows color ran into that of the other virgins, sending a little of warmth and love to them, as they suffered.

Green felt remorse, for being the colors she was says to her self, go ahead let us bleed to death, being matters of the heart. She says take my heart it has been broken and the pain was unbearable. She could feel the weakening in her once sound bodies. The virgins being stripped searched of their life's rhythms and dignity.

The two virgins Green and Yellow have kindred spirits, heart and soul. Yellow grabs the wing of Green, seeing she was depressed and tells her, "Mercy is on our side!" She felt a little better, they fell under the same hat, turning their combo colors Indigo Blue. Making their force stronger, from their sisters pure mind, they both heard their sister Indigo saying, "Have faith sister, have faith," as she lay there limp. Her sisters shared their combo colors giving Indigo a part of themselves, blood donors. Sharing the same fate as they fall wing and wing, if lucky enough to have a wing to hold! Which leads to an even greater power of attachment!

Our next feathered friends will be two pure White Turtledoves; these entities are the symbols of loving kindness and the pure in heart. These doves are named Maya which means Love and Tomora which means: Hope. Our birds will be included as deliverers of things to come, using their special attributes compassion to break the news gently to all those who live in the heart of the deep untamed wilderness. "Secret Teachings," The ability of birds to leave Earth and fly aloft toward the source of light has resulted in their being associated with aspiration, purity, and beauty. Wings were therefore often added to various terrene creatures in an effort to suggest transcendence. Because their habitat was among the branches of the sacred trees in the hearts of ancient forests, birds were also regarded as the appointed messengers of the tree spirits and nature God's dwelling in these consecrated groves, and throughout their clear notes the Gods themselves were said to speak. As the lower world were brought into existence through a generative process, so the dove has been associated with those deities identified with the procreative functions. On account of its gentleness and devotion to its young, the dove was looked upon as the embodiment of the maternal instinct. The dove is also an emblem of the divine will, and signifies the activity of God.

HOLY MOLY!!!!

Mercy says, "Holy Moly!", and called on the South Wind, his turbulence came whistling and twisting in. Mercy said, "Suck it up brother, this is what you were trained for. Get to the Thunder bird quick, as Indigo lights are almost out! Holy Moly, his turbulence wind twisted off into the cosmos."

Thunderbird calls on the Baker Brothers the barn owls small bodies, but great minds to finish up his new pet peeve creation or it would have to be resized, weighed and measured. He instructed the Baker Brothers, be careful, as it is still fragile and in the making. It has begun rising, and we cannot stop now. All creation would fall behind because of the unexpected trip The BUILDER named Bill, The BAKER simply Baker AND THE CANDLE STICK maker named Sticks (BAKER BROTHERS).

They covered the bowl with velvet purple and gold SILK scarf for concealment, the color of royalty the holiest color of cloud nine the certain of concealment.

The Bill brings a SOLID-FOUNDATION. Baker brings FREASHNESS and TENDERNESS and Sticks the FLAME OF DISIRE WHICH HOUSES THE SOUL YET LIGHTENS THE SPIRIT he flickering softly with infinities desires.

The East Winds sounded his trumpets Duet tadadeee the three talents were off to their temple, called Bakerville. The South Wind whistled his wind powers, they where gone in a blink of the Eye.

HANDS OF GOD

The Four Winds had to 'suck up' BROTHERS this is what we were intended for; their powers within. The South Wind gave a whistle the East Wind sounded the trumpet, the North Wind the twelve gong and the West Wind (a- Hoot) then pushed off with their combo wind force powers. Giving the illusion of a violent twisted tornado, they call them HANDS OF GOD!

These deities are the sons of Zeus, they come from the ancient Galaxy of Atlantis the rock of ages, where history begins. East blew his trumpets sending sound vibrations to the Southern Hemispheres, announcing their arrival to the land of (R&R).

CREATION OF COMPANION

Phoenix could hear them coming like b52 bombers. Phoenix was in the process of creating new foams, for the glory of the new heavens. She always puts on her white coat. For the Glory of the Gods. She pulled out of herself a formless blob like pink silly putty, a holy sphere, called the 'Soul Bird's Seed' being the most important aspect. I shall instill green heart, blue mind, red body and yellow for soul. One with keen smell, sight, instincts and one who will listens well. It will be a noble companion, a bird's best friend. She began mixing up her magic, sprinkling blue moon dust on the infant hoping, for a boy, clapping in the air, and dancing around the infant, humming aum and singing the nine holy words. All four were traits blossomed perfectly.

(EMERGENCY)

At that moment the South Wind had arrived first, telling Phoenix that there was a problem back at Seventh Heavens. Phoenix exclaimed as he shed his white coat: "HOLY MOLY!" We need Phoenix's magic power or the entire project would fail, and fall from GRACE. Indigo has been unraveled, her temple is almost stone cold. Call on the Baker Brothers.

HOLY MOLY then disappeared instantly. Arriving back in the Seventh Heaven, with his roaring Blue Thunder and the four golden wind jet powers, a sonic boom hit. She went straight to Temple of Indigo, seeing Sky Blue in solemn prayer, still weeping her color at the door step of her sisters Temple, among Indigo's ruins.

Phoenix swooped up Sky Blue gently, tucking her under a wing. Soothing her with words of comfort, Love is in your heart dwell upon your sisters green temple, bathing her in comforting love. Setting her down softly in the wings of Grace, comfort filled her soul.

SAVING GRACE

Once they arrived at MERCY'S Temple, Mercy had her mouth covered. Thinking in her mind; HAVE MERCY-HAVE MERCY ON THEE. Graces eyes covered with her wings Thinking LET-IT-BE-LET-IT-BE have Mercy ON THEE I plead. Praying that the Phoenix would arrive soon. Their Blue lightning struck the temple walls of Mercy, vibrating their duel healing energy throughout the temple walls. She arrived!

Phoenix and Mercy could see that Alceto had deceived and took advantage of the four virgins. MERCY was pissed that she was struck below the belt in her temple, with her cutthroats, that did the dirty work. Slicing their throats, Alceto is unmerciful, in the hands of ugly!

Yellow was the closest to her lifeless sister, Indigo. It just so happened that some of Yellow's color trickled onto the drying liquid color of her sister, turning Indigo's blood Green, it tingled the feet of green the moment this happened. Indigo's (SAVING-GRACE)! A redeeming feature! Alceto split the scene with her teamster cut throats disappearing with their wicked laughter. Singing their motto - kick them when their down.

Alceto knew very well that she was not to cause any harm to the remaining virgins but she took advantage of them any way. She struck below the belt. When Mercy was away, Alceto became very Merciless and nasty with them. Telling the virgins that they were back in the hands of Ugly, my little pretties! With WICKED pleasure in her witches' laughter.

Alceto knew she had better split the scene for know, leaving with her wicked laughter.

The Phoenix and Mercy were very unhappy, with the undo treatment of Alceto's Needless acts of torment.

TREASURES IN THE HEART

The Phoenix could see that some of Yellow's blood had gotten on Indigo, turning her heart Green; the heart beat of Yellow's soul. Indigo's heartbeat, was very weak but, still beating. Yellow had put life back in her unknowingly, the very color that brings life to the heart of a soul. Mercy was very pleased with the intuitive power of Yellows' saving her sister. (INTUITIVENESS) was born out of the soul of Yellow. Which will play an important roll for all creation in Heaven and on Earth

BAD BLOOD

They now were back in the hands of Mercy; with their heads bowed, wings stretched to the feet of the sister of fate. The virgins still had their mother's unsound blood within them. The BAD BLOODS must GO !

It was now the moment of truth or dare. Mercy had made her mind up. These virgins' souls must be divided in to two halves. We will have to call on our sister, only once more, to do her ugly deeds!

Mercy spoke up saying to Alceto you will have your half WITH HOLES IN THEIR HEARTLESS SOULS. The other half now belongs to Grace, the half with heart. The ball game was back in her hands for one last instant. She was going to put on a show for all to see, that they all would never forget!

Mercy spoke up saying to Alceto, "you will have your half WITH HOLES IN THEIR HEARTLESS SOULS. The other half now belongs to Grace, the half with heart. The ball game was back in her hands for one last instant.

The virgins heads were still bowed, they could only hear the sounds of sharp knives being rung together making an eerie screeching and slicing noises. All Alceto's bat beasts with big drawling teeth they had mini sharp cutting shears crab claw to nip a snip at the heels, of their black claws. To the right of the RED coats only she commanded. She cuts them loose for a little more entertainment.

Once the dust had cleared, with eyes wide open, they could see her Red Dragon, with snorts of fire coming from his mouth and the burning smoke of damnation coming from his nostrils. They could smell foulness in the air growing stronger as he approached with thousands of her demon companions; her mundane cut throat family. This was a once in a life time event and Alceto wanted them all to be there with her, being the center of attraction at the moment!

THE-PIED PIPER

The winds of his hot flames came roaring in with his wicked sounding power tools and the humming of his flute. All eyes where on this destructive force. The simpleton set up the torture racks, unknowing as the are. They stretched their wings to the limit. Mercy says to the seven condemned, "Time to pay the Pied Piper! I'm finished." She calls on the Iron Man. You could hear his band wagon of blades coming with slashing blades, clashing knives and saw blades winding up. The double bladed swords the pied pipers pride and joy, it's his pleasure to divide. You could feel the heat from the hot bladed chariot made of obsidian that looked like the cutting edge of death, with his team of demon sea serpents with mouths the size of a Venus fly trap and a long tongue that looks like the tongue of the red dragons. He releases his serpents to have a piece of the pie, they slither quickly to the feast, tasting with their long forked tongues the sweet taste of death. Leaving razor shape slices on their featherless bodies, hissing with pleasure.

Cut throats bring me the sea salts of Mother Earth and sprinkle a little flavor on The Bad Bloods! The seven screamed silently, with pain and agony. Like in a bad dream! This insanity is for the wicked and the unjust.

Alceto says, your hearts are cold blooded like mine, my little pretty kindred spirit! With chilling wicked laughter, your hemispheres will be divided (RED Coats and The Blue Coats); red coats breed condemnation, and the Blue coats which will free the souls. Red coats will never fly again in the realm of the celestials. Time to walk the plank! Take the heat! The GOOD the BAD and the UGLY! Splitting of the fine feathers, severing of souls.

The temple filled, with hot orange roaring flames and the smoke rose red as the pied piper bring out his cutting edge of death. The swords of broken hearts! Eager to do the dirty work of Mercy's wicked side. "Have Mercy!" His blades wound up the slashing and the ringing of blade surrounded the condemned, He picks Indigo first bottoms up! I believe!! As soon as the last drop of colored blood fell, the saw was revved loudly for a little added entertainment. Her blood fell Indigo turning to powder, ash and salt. They all could see that Indigo was a true Blue spirit, there cold hearts said Oh hells' bells another one bites the dust. Same was true for Sky Blue, Yellow and Green! But Dodora and her favored daughters a had malice in their hearts, their blood fell into sand and the salt of time.

TIME

Stick saying these things take (TIME), as they're flying HOLY-MOLY, Covering his mouth--- He hit the nail on the head! Putting a spike in the timing of things, he was waxed by leaking out something that would control MANKIND and all inhabitants. Creating TIME before its time. The Builder was floored, the baker was Flatten; I hope this does not put a crack in the ANCIENT OAK Bowl of the thunder birds. Baker tucks the bowl tight.

The Bill says, now that it's out! (IT'S JUST A MATTER OF TIME!!)The North Wind appeared bring the twelve gongs, before their time, holy moly oh brothers! What have we done! Well let's seize opportunity and use it in the making of our creation, we cannot waste his energy. We will have to borrow some sand from the sand man, and we will have to figure out what divides lightness and darkness. How about using it for just seven (DAYS), Lets call it the "(seven DAYS OF CREATION) Sticks hitches a ride on the North Wind and they head to the ancient galaxy of Atlantis the rock of ages, so we can have the sands of time back in time for the next coming event.

BAKERSVILLE

They had arrived at their cozy Temple.

The Baker warmed up the oven, Bill got his wooden nails and his special wooded oak hammer. Being the hammer head of the (PET) project would begin first. HE nailed it. The Sticks would bring the soft music, a softly light fragrance candles, of Jasmine, they lit his temple. Baker got out his huge bread pan made of PURE WHITE GOLD for creating the best. Baker buttered it, slapped it, and then capped it. Of course the best is yet to come! The BUNS in the oven. Baker keeps a watchful eye on the project.

Bill was of to visit two soft silhouettes. The two kindred spirits, EBB AN FLOW the minor silhouette Moons, the polarity opposes, the balancing scales.

TWO MOONS

FLOW the soft black sister moon, the keeper of the WHITE pearls essence of ebb. And EBB brother moon, the soft neon white, the keepers of the BLACK pearl essence. Two powerful deities, the white and black tail deer known as (The Two Moons) dual kindred spirits in the expanse of the Otter Limit. The Bill arrived, for a visit at Two Moons. Let me call EBB to share in the balanced, good company. FLOW rattled her birdcage and then opened the cage door. Out hopped the Messengers (the Love Birds) the birds of loving friendships, and the center pieces of companionship. Brother, moon will be here in a Hoot coming from the west side.

31

They all heard him coming, on his winged Harley. He always comes in hip hopping as if in a horse race. As he stopped, giving it three revs for the spirits of the holy ghosts.

What's cooking? Who's baking? And who's in the makings? Yin says, would you like a cookie Honey? Nut Chocolate chip! Bakers ask GOT PURPLE MILK?

Baker explains, back at home on cloud nine we were creating the best companion, for the Seventh Heavens. HE will have Telepathy, devotion, dedication, unconditional love; he will become the animal friend they can count on. It will have instinctive powers way beyond all others. He will also fill the hearts of lonely soul, will be a protector, and a Stewart to serve and serve well.

The project was put on hold, along with the creation of Mother Earth because of three tyrants, and now we need help from outside sources, to complete the mission Yang, asks how we can help to get the balls rolling? Baker says; do you still have Jim Bob the otter and his pups around ? The big daddy of like a rock, the keeper of silver bullets band and the silver lining of puppy power? We do! Do you think he's gig would be willing, to share some of his special silver bullet thrusters and the silver lining of puppy love?

They all went in support; of "get-er-Done" Baker rode on the back Yin. Jack had some scookum bean stalks in his garden of silver otter pups and bean spouts. Every bean has its day, a timely matter of chance. Once they explained he was more than willing to donate some pup power!

Then Bill gave a nod, hoot, and a whistle and a Thank YOU, Thank you very much!!! Two Moons invited them back once their mission impossible was completed.

CREATION OF COMPANION

All seeing-eyes watch with anticipation. His physical ability will be superior to man tall-tale traits. The noble companion for humanity, willing to (SERVE WITH LOVE). The honest, the dedicated, the devoted just willing to please! It will have unconditional love for the master, the perfect example for Seventh Heaven to follow. He will search and seek out, rescue and protect betwixt the zenith and beyond the cosmos...His instincts will guide him, the forerunner that will hold the torch of creation.

Phoenix picked up four cedar sticks; it's to have four legs with feet and toes, so it can move twice as fast, a good idea. Now that he had all the right ingredients, he placed them carefully in his holy mixing bowl. The Phoenix then pulled out nine red, white and blue tail feathers etched in gold for patriotism. His white doves wanted to "SERVE WITH LOVE". They sprinkle a tough of class onto the prospect.

EMERGENCY AT THE TWILIGHT ZONE...HOLY MOLY!!!

Phoenix calls on the Baker Brothers the barn owls small bodies, but great minds to finish up his new pet peeve creation or it would have to be resized, weighed and measured. He instructed the Baker Brothers, be careful, as it is still fragile and in the making, it has begun rising and we cannot stop now. All creation would fall behind because of the unexpected trip. The BUILDER named Bill, the BAKER, simply Baker AND THE CANDLE STICK MAKER named Sticks (BAKER BROTHERS).

They covered the bowl with velvet purple and gold SILK scarf for concealment, the color of royalty the holiest color of cloud nine, the curtain of concealment.

The Bill brings a SOLID-FOUNDATION. Baker brings FREASHNESS and TENDERNESS and Sticks the FLAME OF DESIRE WHICH HOUSES THE SOUL YET LIGHTENS THE SPIRIT, he flickering softly with infinity's desires.

The East Winds sounded his trumpets Duet tadadeee the three talents were off to their temple, called Bakersville. The South Wind whistled his wind powers, they were gone in a blink of the eye.

TIME

Stick saying things take (TIME), as they're flying HOLY-MOLY, covering his mouth-- He hit the nail on the head! Putting a spike in the timing of things, he was waxed by leaking out something that would control MANKIND and all inhabitants. Creating TIME before its...The Builder was floored, the Baker was Flattened; I hope this does not put a crack in the ANCIENT OAK Bowl of the thunder birds. Baker tucks the bowl tight.

Then Bill says, now that it's out! (IT'S JUST A MATTER OF TIME!!) The North Wind appeared bring the twelve gongs, before their time. What have we done! Well let's seize the opportunity and use it in the making of our creation, we cannot waste his energy. We will have to borrow some sand from the sand man and we will have to figure out what divides lightness and darkness. How about using it for just seven (DAYS), Let's call it the "SEVEN DAYS OF CREATION". Sticks hitches a ride on the North Wind and they head to the ancient galaxy of Atlantis the rock of ages, so we can have the sands of time back in time for the next coming event.

BAKERSVILLE

They had arrived at their cozy Temple.

The Baker warmed up the oven, Bill got his wooden nails and his special wooded oak hammer. Being the hammer head of the (PET) project would begin first. HE nailed it. The Sticks would bring the soft music, a softly light fragrance candles of Jasmine. They lit his temple. Baker got out his huge bread pan made of PURE WHITE GOLD for creating the best. Baker buttered it, slapped it, and then capped it. Of course the best is yet to come! The BUN'S in the oven. Baker keeps a watchful eye on the project.

Bill was off to visit two soft silhouettes. The two kindred spirits, EBB AND FLOW the minor silhouette. Moons, the polarity opposes the balancing scales.

TWO MOONS

FLOW the soft black sister moon, the keeper of the WHITE pearls, essence of ebb. And EBB brother moon, the soft neon white, the keepers of the BLACK pearl essence. Two powerful deities, the white and black tail deer known as (The Two Moons) dual kindred spirits in the expanse of the Otter Limit. The Bill arrived, for a visit at Two Moons. Let me call EBB to share in the balanced, good company. FLOW rattled her birdcage and then opened the cage door. Out hopped the Messengers (the Love Birds) the birds of loving friendships, and the center pieces of companionship. Brother, moon will be here in a Hoot coming from the West side.

They all heard him coming, on his winged Harley. He always comes in hip-hopping as if in a horse race. As he stopped, giving it three revs for the spirits of the holy ghosts.

What's cooking? Who's baking? And Who's in the makings? Yin says, would you like a cookie Honey? Nut Chocolate Chip! Baker asks GOT PURPLE MILK?

Baker explains, back at home on cloud nine we were creating the best companion for the Seventh Heavens. HE will have Telepathy, devotion, dedication, unconditional love; he will become the animal friend they can count on. It will have instinctive powers way beyond all others. He will also fill the hearts of lonely souls, will be a protector, and a Stewart to serve and serve well.

The project was put on hold, along with the creation of Mother Earth because of three tyrants, and now we need help from outside sources to complete the mission. Yang asks how can we help to get the balls rolling? Baker says; do you still have Jim Bob the otter and his pups around? The big daddy of like a rock, the keeper of silver bullets band and the silver lining of puppy power? We do! Do you think he's gig would be willing, to share some of his special silver bullet thrusters and the silver lining of puppy love?

They all went in support of: of "Get-er-Done" Baker rode on the back of Yin. Jack had some skoocum bean stalks in his garden of silver otter pups and bean sprouts. Every bean has its day, a timely matter of chance. Once they explained he was more than willing to donate some pup power!

Then Bill gave a nod, hoot, and a whistle and Thank YOU, Thank you very much!!! Two Moons invited them back once their mission impossible was completed.

Back in Bakersville, Baker waited patiently for the arrival of his brothers and the pup powers. The new creation was finishing up; Baker began smelling a new scent. It was quite unusual, he smelt like cut green grass, and wet dog hair! The North Wind sounded the chimes, the twelve gongs of creation, rang. The stars were set in motion; it was time for the year of the dog to be born. Bakers say, come on baby come on, with anticipation! He had ready the holy waters, the anointing oil myrrh, the twelve candle sticks lit and the stones of suffering and pain arranged around the whelping table.

The Baker Brothers arrive at that very moment, just in time for the delivery of the new creation. They watch with anticipation as Baker opens the oven doors.

He gently opened the oven, popped it out of the pan pop, pop. The North Wind blew the breath of life into the new soul. East placed some warm liquid sunshine next to it for warmth, East Wind red rose petals for unconditional love, and West Wind some soul food. As it dried it began whimpering like a puppy. Its' whimpers became stronger with every breath. The Baker Brothers sat back with eyes wide open watching closely. The creation began growing, with sounds of squeaking balloon would sound.

The whimpering became a rolling bark, a whinney, then a rolling bark, a whimper, a whinney, a bark, still growing with every sound vibration. The brothers began laughing hysterically, they roared on the floor with laughter the poor thing had been a bit mixed up in the ingredients. He was part horse, part dog, and part human with ears as big as life. He had the strength of the mighty horse. By now his voice and size had grown to that of the Trojan horse. It had become quite an unusual creation! Baker says, Greetings, Wild-Thing!!! It whinnied a big deep hello.

The Baker Brothers' realization hit, they quit laughing. Silence filled their temple. Then Bill says it's a wooden horse, with built in assets!!! The sticks say it's a dog to be man's best friend and stand by his side!!! The Baker says, I think it came out nothing less than perfect. I see potential written all over it!!! We'll let Phoenix name it. Let's prepare it for the journey.

MEET PHOENIX

The Baker Brother bathed him in holy water, anointed him with myrrh, and smuggled him with sweet grass. He shined like the sun himself. The covered him with the velvet purple scarf for concealment. They all hopped on his enormous back. The brothers gave a whistle; pet peeve instinctively flew to the door steps of the Phoenix. Ding-dong from the North Wind, a warm wind swept in from the South Wind, opening the crystal palace doors. They approached the throne, and then knelt down out of reverent respect with his white dove of peace. Pet Peeve sniffed a feather up his nose made him sneeze, blowing his cover, before the Baker Brothers had a chance to explain! Bad news for someone who is trying to make a good first impression.

Oh my God, what in the Sam hell is this? A FREAKIN' HALF-BREED!!! The Baker Brothers were shaking in their boots, dead serious with a lump in their crawls. He started laughing himself, they let him laugh for a few seconds then they joined in before it was done the entire palace was vibrating with humor. This creation will have to do. There's not enough time to re-create it. We will name it DOG-GONE-HORUS. He sill have to rely on his inner strengths and talents to pull this off.

Dog-Gone-Horus speaks for himself; "BIG IS BAD, when it comes to balls and I got them THANK YOU VERY MUCH, I stand on one paw, it's enough to see me through, to dig deep "My foot hold" My stability, My foot print in the sand, I will become "pure stardom" I'll earn my three legs title. I have the power to believe and I can dream!"

"I will be a noble companion willing to "serve with love" the honest dedicated. Devotee willing to please the unconditional lover of my Masters. I'll become cosmic wonderer, a dog star. My physical attributes will, out run birds four to two. Walks the tight rope and seek and search out where they leave off. My senses are sharper and keen; I'll become the four runners, who hold the torch of this creation."

ORDERS

Pheonix speaks, Dog-Gone Horus, left ear stood straight up. Lend an ear and listen to the voice of reason. His ears perfectly designed for acoustics. He hears the silent trumpet sound. Your mission is to bring back the nine missing pieces to the puzzlement, to finish the Perfect Plan. We will give you red roller skates they laced the skates with confidence, have skates will travel like greased lightning! You're to seek out the untouchables, and touch the untamed, in the wilderness of the cosmos. Go to the Galaxy of Knodea. Round up the power houses and return with the feather weight spheres in their purest forms.

BEWARE OF THE BLACK HOLES you will first feel a thick static in the air, your hair will stand on end. If you don't change course you'll be swallowed up by the oceans of Alceto's darkness; Called the Dead Sea Scrolls. Where the dead souls gather and feast upon themselves. The white dove's claws curled.

Take your gifts, use and wear them well!!! Bill you have the silver bullet thrusters and the puppy powers? I do! Give him a round. Sticks you have the flints and skate oil? I do! Sock it to him! ON your marks, get set!! GO! DOG-GONE HORUS GO! The four winds blew their forces onto the platform under Horus's feet, they were gone like greased lightning.

The Phoenix thought, experiments lead to new discoveries! It felt good that the first creation was off. The Phoenix smiled with laughter at the clown we have created for the good of all! And was pleased, yet unsatisfied. The Phoenix whispered to itself "GET-R-DONE" my faithful friend! As they watched a streamer of color coming from the tail wind, then gone into the oblivion of the cosmos and to the Galaxy of Knodea.

GALAXY OF KNODEA

Dog-gone-Horus left jaded but returned trumpet, he was requested to visit the Galaxy of Knodea the enchanted planet of Golden Means, in the Valley of Blossoms. Orchids lined the golden pastures, to the Valley of the Lotus Beauties, roses lined the meadows with silk kissed Opal skies, on to a bed of blue grass pastures. Once there you, will find Romeo and Juliet the Adam and Eve of paradise. They have the fragile feather weights needed to finish the Seventh Heavens. They must be captured with the iron butterfly net of faith, before they tough the blue grasses of paradise.

They call her Florence of Arabians which means bouquet of flowered beauty, she's of the purest bred Equines in the Galaxy.

Florence was pleasing to the eye and warming to the heart and soothing to the soul. She had a cosmic purple halo surrounding her beauty. With her black light mustang mane and tail that glowed in the dark and light.

The beauty queen of the dawning of Aquarius, the Phoenix of her plant. She wore her talent well, breath-taking, glorious. She raises to the music of the morning doves "coo" saying arise our beauty Queen arise. She awakes before the dusk of dawn, her lightened spirit moves her to the bubbling brook of life, the holy waters of the Black Light Mustangs. She moves to the still waters, as smooth as a glass, and she could see her own flawless image.

Florence slips into the waters with out a ripple as she descends she begins humming the sound vibration AUM, the waters begin swaying to her music. The black light waters begin teaming with life. The Bubbling colors rouse, popping the scent of the day. The black light waters moved into the colors of the Aurora-Borealis, sending colored lights up into their Indigo velvet skies, just before the dawn.

Florence emerges with the kindred spirit of Eo's the Swan, daughter of dawn, with her chariot of White Tigers, announcing the coming of the Sun and their extinction. Dawn bursts through with the dawning of Aquarius, the birth of MORN. Florence carries on the back the saddle bags of the Great Square Ladle or the Great wall of Water the Zenith of Life.

The fillies of hope are waiting for the arrival of dawn, at the waters edge. In high hopes of being the pick of the new dawning day, with their feather quill mane and tails, still a part of their tender characters. The bold the beautiful challengers of the untamed spirit. Hidden talents, the spark of individuality the budding of the lotus to each its own destiny, let their spirits run with confidence!

Eo's lassos seven of the best for the glory of the rising Sun with golden rope that binds. They gallop with merriment, bucking, snorting and kicking their spirits high fallowing Eo's. Chasing the Ray-fleers of darkness away, as they disappear into the horizon. Flora glances to see the swirling pink clouds of appeasement shine through; she whispers amen three times, warmth filled her soul with pleasing pleasure.

Florence runs like Wind River, back to her morning glory temple. She's greeted loudly by her twelve peacock guard dog. They strut their stuff around the garden gates with their all watchful eyes, their virtue. Mesmerizing all who look upon their beauty. If Florence was a bird she would be the Peacock.

Her Mothers of deliverance await her with a nod, a snort, a whinny and a kiss to her beautiful full cheeks. They crown her with the stars sapphire gemstone, the deliverance of let freedom ring. The red spotted mare, called Desire with a white and red striped mane and tail. The mare of fertility, love making, immaculate conceptions, birth and courage. The White mare called Innocence, with her Golden Fleece mane and tail, she's the sweet mothers milk;" for the babes", nurturing, growth, experience and ancient wisdom. The Blue, grey, mare called Karma, with her black light silk spider webbed mane and tail. She rules all truth, prophecies, past lives, life and death. She corrals all in her webs that weave, the realm of the dead, black holes and all karma!

These four goddesses bring the flag of truths! The Red the White and The Blue, and the stars, and stripes of experience and wisdom. The Black Light Mustangs of deliverance!

O beautiful for spacious skies,
For amber ways of grain,
For purple mountains majesties
Above the fruited plans!

America! America!
God shed his grace on thee
And crown thy good with sisterhood
from sea to shining sea!

O beautiful for patriots dream
That sees beyond the years
Thine alabaster cities gleam
Undimmed by human tears!

America! America!
God shed his grace on thee
And crown thy good with brotherhood
From sea to shining sea!

The white morning doves descend, bringing to serve with love attitudes, as the atmosphere begins warming Golden Means. The mares adore, cherish, worship and adorn her golden heart, she's the most beautiful beauty of all the land, and admired by all.

The Red mare Desire prepares a place passionately, for the mile high rising of Adam and Eve's paradise. They are the chasm of love on the planet of Golden Means. Desire weaves a coat of love red, white, and blue roses into the shape of the heart chakra. She laid it across her long back. Desire decks the thresh hold with laurel for peace, purple orchids for harmony, blue morning glories for hope Ylang Ylang for love and mistletoe for union at the center, for the approaching love affair.

The black mare Karma prepares the path to the temple floor, a circle of obsidian and pearls boarders the symbol (AUM) made of pure jade the protective force that guards the heart, of suffering and pain. She pours clear quartz liquid crystal, amongst the stones, giving it a transparent elusion as the light shined up from the center glowing ever brighter as the morning moved on.

The White mare Innocents lavishly adorns Florence with precious cut gem stones. She put a pyramid terra curved like the crescent moon made with black and white diamonds, at the point the sapphire gem, the eye of all reasoning.

They begin with her black hooves, a sound foundation. They shawl her with White gold shoes, nailed with nine pearl spikes, for their humaneness. Then they pierce her hooves with the seven times seven cut gemstones from the rhythms of the cosmos. Layering them with the seven sacred colors of the Aurora-Borealis they glistened with color, like Dorothy's shoes from the Wizard of Oz.

Innocence bathes her with motherly loving kindness, nurturing her with words of adoration and encouraging her with poetry, psalms and hymns as she weaves virtue in to her hair. Innocence finish up with the Mylee flower, the most sacred lotus of the planet. The flower with a thousand petals, and the anointing oil of purity. It holds the essences of faith within its mesmerizing beauty. The top of her tail the summit, she weaved the yellow ribbon of hope and faith, from the old oak tree, binding the forces.

Her mane her traditional black light shoe string strands. (Her planet's personal trade mark) Innocence braided and beaded tiny white pearls that trickled down her stream line neck which gave it a neon soft luster. Tipped with heart shaped rose quartz crystals that flickered and lit up to the sounds of her own celestial making. Their queen is now ready for her song and dance, leaving tickle, color ,flavor, lascivious beauty and a heavenly scent in the wake of her presence. Her mane flowed down her stream line back touching her tail, electrifying it with cosmic colors. Lighting the sacred torch of the subtle Aurora-Borealis within, a rare sight to behold only for the privileged. She wore it well!

Her morning doves coo at the sight of such a magnificent beauty.

She was ripe with lascivious, extravagates, and merriment her holy temple prepared for his arrival. The Sagittarian stallion, Jacob, is the gem stone guardian from the Valley of Precious Gems. His Stone Hedge Temple houses the Rosetta Stone the most sacred, sought after treasure of the land. When floras spring comes, all gather around Stone Hedge and celebrate the coming of spring Flora the beginning, and Jacob the harvest, they are the alpha and omega of the Planet of Golden Means the most cherished couple on the planet. He had the perfect body of a stallion, the torso of muscular man, golden locks of hair and the wings of a golden eagle. The man with the magic hands." The HORSE-MAN" He's the guardian of LOVE, and the treasures of the heart chakra, and cherished memories.

He rises at high noon, when Flora is in her full glory; He opens his golden eyes, and is greeted with a smile and a kiss. Jacob begins gently caressing her neck, messaging her brisket with passionate gentle strokes of loving kindness. Kissing her forehead softly with his Elvis lips, as he tastes his way down to her soft nose; her G spot. He says, "My love what beautiful nostril hairs you have" and that velvet nose is to die for, "the bee's knees", she blushes. Her aroma stimulates his taste buds for more. He begins nibbling and nipping her ears and neck; she tosses her head as if in a poetic dance, he then grazes upon her juice body of virtues. He thrives on pleasing his lover, nuzzling and kissing her, moaning with tasteful pleasure. The man with the magic hands! He woos her with his touch.

Adoring her with cherished love songs, hearts begin to throb with passion and desire lights its fire. He strokes her softly and gently as he works his way down her stream line soft back, her colors changing beneath his finger tips toughing her with passionate loving strokes. Mares love the touch of man hands on them. As soon as she is tickled pink, he unties the yellow ribbon from the old oak tree, it softly falls like silk ribbon around her sparkling hooves. The fruit is ripe for the picking as they indulge in the fine art of love making, working their way to the crown of full glory, the wild thing, the climax. Absorbing every humble moment spent! Reaching passions peck the summit of nirvana! The Mylee flower! He gently unties the rest of the yellow ribbon of hope, then takes the sacred flower and lifts it into the air, blesses it, and then offers it to Flora. Then he lifts his wings and hands in praise to the master minds and in a deep Elvis voice says THANK YOU THANK YOU VERY MUCH for the gifts bestowed on me!

WHITE STONE MOUNTAIN

They then run like the wind to the Purple Mountain pecks of White Stone Mountain, where the peaks are made of jagged ivory tusks, a gift from the BIG ONE and the nine crystals colored mountain pecks sacred temples of Koomba the Unicorn. It's Called

ATUMRA-"WHERE HEART MIND BODY AND SOUL manifest". They arrive at the summit called "Eagles' Peak".

They come to appease the mystic unicorn. His body is of the horse, with the head of a deer, the feet of the elephant and the tail of a boar, a deep bellowing voice and a single black horn two cubits in length that stands out of his forehead. He's elusive; once in a blue moon you could see him on the rock cliffs of White Stone Mountain. He lives behind the Tumble water falls of the Aurora–Borealis, the falls to enlightenment at the heart of the planet. The Emperor of the ray-seekers and the golden light, the Stewart of purity. He's a ferocious beast, a protector of chivalrous, purity and innocent. His noble character honors the 'mares of deliverance' the birth rights to us all.

Florence prepares a bed of golden fleece for Koomba, and a bed of roses letting them fall softly where they may around her. With her black light beauty, color, flavor, obviousness, wit and charm, he could smell the scent of Florence in the air; he approaches the falls with caution. He spots his blue beauty, his heart skips a beat, and passion melts his heart. It's time to replenish his spirit with the light of love, the only fuel he needs for his immortality.

He holds his breath, takes the fathom leaps of faith though the colored falls. The falls freeze over, but the colors still moving as a mirage upon his still waters his cavern lit up like the sun, being made of solid white gold and ivory and pyramids of every gem imaginable! The most longed after virtues of immortality.

Her black light beauty shined through, as she puts on the Ritz, bringing out her true colors. The unicorn approaches with reverence, crouching besides her, laying his head next to her heart. She circumvents him as she pet and pats him with tender loving care. Her black light beauty lures him into a trance, then he falls asleep, the only time he rests his soul. His day dreams of being with Florence in his valley of peace and paradise.

Romeo approaches with respect; he nods, bows, and then blesses the holy waters with the nine holy words. He holds the shield of hearts made of solid emerald with topaz leaves that boarders the edges. He holds the shield to protect his heart from the rays of the sun. It's so bright it transmutes, sending holy light upon itself. It was so bright he had to wear Elton John sun glasses! He draws upon his bronze saddle bags. He brings treasures from his heart, uncut gems. He pulls out his pious stones, that which pleases the Gods. He blows on them with a blessing as an offering and slips them into the waters without a ripple.

Romeo then pulls out his great square ladle made of clear quartz crystals and the red rubies of desire. As soon as he slips the ladle into the holy waters of White Stone Mountain began humming their vibrations and shined their colors. Then mountain then speaks "I AM THE GREAT I AM" Romeo bows with a rolling hand gesture. Romeo then steps into the waters, hoof deep. He became one with the waters. He gently cut into the waters, with his ladle of desire and drawing up the diamonds in the rough, soldiers of immortality. He carefully transfers them into the Holy Grail cup made of solid gold. The mountain came alive like a pipe organ, the seven mountain peaks danced up and down to the rhythm of the forest canopy, whole lot of shaken going on.

He slowly retreats. Saying AMEN nine times, then the rustling of the big one began calling I'm the Gem Stone Guardian Atumra the heart, mind, body, and soul of the forests. The majestic moose oracle, an aromatic cedar tree, made of rugged moose horn and sacred white tail deer antler, betwixt the celestial skies. It had long lichen moss that looks like locks of golden hair; that of father time. They dripped like tears of golden joy coming from their stout antler limbs. They clank and clapped their antlers, swaying to the music with singing pleasure. Then says; I am the alpha and omega of all the forests to come, the rock of ages, the granddaddy of the bones to Mother Earth, the majestic ruler of all forests and gemstones. His trunk began vibrating the Aum the tips of his horns lit up like a Christmas tree. Lightning flashed the colors of the rainbow shooting from his finger tips electrifying the entire forest.

The four universal golden eagles, from cloud nine descended on the mighty limbs of Atumra, picked the stout limbs, bringing the power of breath to life. You could hear their wings reproaching, with the sound of roaring horse hooves, brings the falls back to life! Romeo gives Florence a soft whinnie signaling her to make her move.

Florence slips out from under the unicorn, giving the beast a kiss, then laid a dozen purple roses at his big feet. They bow, he gives a whistle, she whinnies and then they give the Hi- Ho- silver stance. Then run like the wind back to their blue grasses of paradise to greet the foals of hope. Where the black light mustangs live, thrive and grow.

The doves of peace accompany Romeo and Juliet; they sweep open the bronze saddle bags and lift the Holy Grail cup up into the celestial skies of opaline, to the pink seed clouds of infinity. They strike the golden cords of the harp. The angels sing. They descend as feather weights, being tickled pink. Courage is installed and gifts granted.

The touch the blue grasses of paradise, and manifest into tiny elector-lights of buzzing light the hummingbird, the size of a mustard seed. They vibrate to their own rhythms VAM with swift wings and black light feather quill mane and tails and a single yellow feather faith from the Iron Butterflies. Their smallest voice will become one of the mightiest.

Florence could see that all was well with the infant hummers and the spirited black light mustang foals. The abundance of love fills her heart with spiritual bliss and pleasing delight. She snorts big Thanks, for her cup that runneth over. She bows in honor of her loved ones, blow them all a kiss sending her scent, color and flavor to all. A whole hearted whinny for all souls Day and the blessings from White Stone Mountain and a sincere amen to the master minds. She squalls as she runs like Wind River back to her flower garden.

Florence loops gracefully back to her garden grove, of her own creation, her pride and joy. Thinking to herself "We are the lucky ones" She's greeted by the all seeing eyes of the peacocks the guard dogs to the third eye and Florence's extravagant flower garden of fulfillment. Their hypnotizing beauty is carried with elegance, grace and suffocated extravagance, pride, and beauty. They announce the coming of Florence, guests or intruders with their large loud voice. If Florence was a bird she would have been the Peacock.

She has fragile fairies that live and thrives in her garden the size, shape and color of a Robin egg. Her string of pearls that move thought her garden groves. They must always touch each other at all times, their life force energy. They worship the ground she walks on gobbling up her aroma. She moves to the heart beat of her garden, a lush grove of budding color.

She approaches her alter, the fountain of life with reverent respect, she kneels down with a dozen red roses one for each sign of the zodiac and multitude of Purple Heart Roses for all of the fallen soldiers. Her alter pentacle a broken heart made of a solid red ruby with a tiger eye in the center of it. Its heart beat glows yellow with each pulsating beat. Baboom Baboom. The foundation is a thousand fallen arrows the broken hearts of cupid. The double tip, made of obsidian, the shaft made of red garnet white pearls and blue indigo the red white and blue flag of freedom rings. And the tail made of the yellow feathers of faith... The double blades of savored attachments, and the stones of sorrow and pain. The liquid emerald green waters push up from the center with every beat, falling down over the crying eye of the tiger, the well spring of life.

She then picks up the Purple Heart Roses, lifting them to the heavens, blesses them for their cherished moments, for all the fallen loved ones that lives in her heart. The alter beats to the rhythm of the solar plexus of (RA) She picks a rose petal for each fallen loved one, then picks a pearls from her string of pearls and gentle releases them into the emerald waters. Giving all tears of remorse and joys back to karma, the GOOD, the Bad and the ugly flowed down the stream of life to the valley of peace. Beyond the threshold of existence endless it may be, ecstasy awaits thee just you wait and see! The Liberty-Bells ring and her wind songs sing! "Let freedom ring!" She lets go....

She then pulls out her cherished water spout made of pure amethyst, and mothers of pearl, handed down to her by her grandmother Grace. She gives thanks to the healing waters. She then takes a cool drink from her spout of immortality. Then she pours the waters of life onto her flower garden of lasciviousness and beauty.

Her world is set into motion, with the purest blessing bestowed, she's given Grace, The path which leads to enlightenment, the power to lead the spirits, and rule the mind. She would select the perfect orchids of desire, gardenias of passion and the, Ylang Ylangs the flower powers of love in yin and yang.

In honor of Romeo her soul mate, she arranges the most perfect bouquet of lushes colors. Aphrodisiac scented the air with Ylang Ylang the pentacle, of gentle loving kindness. Her doves of peace descend on the throne of Harmony, saying with their coos of courtship. Our kingdom come, our will be done, on earth as it is in heaven. Flora loves the arrival of the doves. Simply one's delight!

Her song birds sing, looking to the setting sun of purple haze and the pink clouds of appeasement, over their blue grass pastures of paradise for her Renaissance man the man with the hands momma! The Sagittarian he has the strength of the centaur, the Archer, the son of Jupiter, the master of possibility, the ruler of the laws of attraction. He's a delicious man of flavor, a free loving and a far reaching spirit. He has Courage of a comet and the spirit of a cosmic warrior, the leader of his class. He was a master of many virtues, Marshall art's his Olympic game, his num-chucks cut through the wind with a swift tone all their own. He wears his talent well, a Black belt of high honor, and has benevolent respect for the saints! He's a lover of poetry, with a joyous nature, desires of a warrior's strength, passions peak and the bidding of true love, the summit of his glory! He had magnetism and was idolized by his virtues. He was the Magistrate of loving kindness.

The apple of his eye and the tenderness in his heart is in the abode of the babes his precious black light mustangs, the shining lights of tender loving care. Grateful to be the godfather to all their free loving souls. He knows time is of the essence, before their set free with the wind into the vast world of wonder! Prepared to set them free to run like wind river to their destines.

Archery, his power house, his cutting edge of attraction, his eagle eye, and sharp impacts, cutting to the heart. He was the first warrior to take a broken arrow, cut him to the heart, and the many that fallowed his lead, He has apathy for all the fallen soldiers, he laid thousands of arrows at the foot of halter of broken hearts, "Heart Break hotel" His endeavor to be the mightiest warrior of the heart, free love and lost lover! He blesses the moments spent, then sets the arrows free!

The magical mid-night hour the clock strike twelve; twelve gongs from the North Wind, the East Wind sounded his trumpet, the South Wind gave the whistle, the West Wind, three hoots!

Then a reverberation began rumbling louder then her soft impulse. A mighty force the roaring of hooves began. ("The Black Light Mustang") (the mothers of deliverance)Their majestic powers push forth. They break the wind and ride waves and split the flames! ("The Mothers of deliverance") their power houses, their untamed spirits. Next the coachmen's team followed by the nine simpletons the work horses. Then the ocean of sailing seahorses come rushing in with the legendary (Black Light Mustangs). Hundreds of black lights mustangs followed the coachmen's lead. Then thousands of soldiers, and support groups for the cosmic cause! They burst forth through the Great Square with the powers of cosmic spirit, the blue thunder strikes, and the comic fire's stirred; the water falls of the Aurora Borealis came gushing forth, followed by the mares of deliverance.

His Juliet had been abducted by the Hickory Dickey, leader of "Ignorance, with his chariot of enormous black grizzly bears, the bearer of mental pain and unjust suffering of others! The dog -gone horus told Romeo that he could seek out and find his lost lover. That's what I was created for. Hold your horses Romeo I'll need (K an-9) we will make a pack. The coachmen gave a whistle, and a Hoot, calling on Hoot and the west wind to assist him. Out of the darkness you could see a swirling dust storm coming, and your could hear the great Horned Owl calling He's deep vibrating tone saying, (GIVE A HOOT) his motto. Hoot arrives with his west wind, the Dog-gone Horus Nods as all do as a greeting to the planet. These four forces teamed up with turbulent wind power, gave them the cutting edge to thieves of the heart. They gave a nod, snort, whistle and a hoot, they where gone with the turbulence of there majestic gale force West Wind.

The coachmen's intuitiveness, instinct, time and power found her, but that's another story.

DOG-GONE HORUS

Dog-Gone- Horus realized that he was a bit mixed up with other species. When he met two kindred spirits, one was called (K) and the other call (9) coupled up as (K9).They where the perfect pet.

Chaps my hide and twists my whiskers, my tong and lips are too thick, it slows up my smooth talking, I have Huge choppers bulky and ugly. I crave green grass milk shake. Know I see why the Phoenix covered my stinking feet with red roller skates! How embarrassing, human feet suck they stumble and are slow, although my red roller skates moved like greased lighting though the cosmos. My foot steps are that of the human race; mine are to be by their side, in the sands of time!

And my body, the size of the trogon horse, gave me a majestic power the size of the horse, and their strength of their team... I'm supposed to set low to the terrestrial ground for scent. MY ears enormous for hearing the word well, but these ears clap like the tail of the beaver. They were to be a fashionable sized, for hearing my inner guides, and listening to my instincts, He did give me a sensitive human heart and a tender foot!

PASSIONS PEAK

Dog- gone-Horus began whimpering about his short comings ands imperfections then he started balling like a baby. Saying in a tearful voice, I won't to be like you. (9) Licks his tears with apathy, compassion and pity saying; we do have our own Baker Brothers, the beaver brothers of the ponds of metamorphose. Leave it to the beavers! They have the sticks and stones that can set you free from the bondage of desire! We could make an appointment and get you a makeover. Dog- gone-Horus's left ear stood straight up, (9) still licking his tears away. (ARE YOU SERIOUS)!!! He felt flames of desire, the sparks that drive us on, his "PASSIONS PEAK" he blushes red with desire.

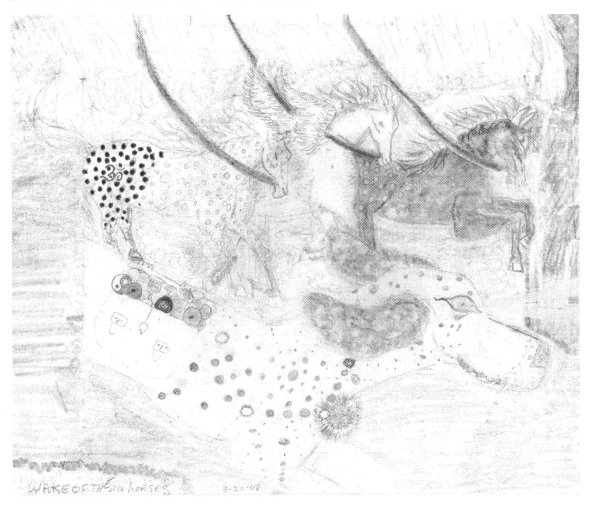

They lead him to the ponds immortality," he emerged triumphant! (THE COACHMEN) The coachmen burst forth through the birthing gates, triumphant, sound, proud, a purebred, a true blue beautiful beast the Dalmatians. His budding soul emerges with his true colors shining though. His coat pattern luminous neon white with blue spots of thoughts covering his beautiful body and the code of ethics tattooed on him. His tail the traditional white whippet tail, with cosmic shoestring colors that shooting from his cosmic tailwind. His jumbo ears take hath and listen well! And keen sight for capturing insight, and experiences. He lets his talents shine through as he sings his song of noble tales.

His hidden treasure for humanity to unravel, and the mystery of mans best friend!

Their realm their universe the untouchables and the untamed, the challengers of the deep, the strong, the rough, and tough the hard to bluff the seas of life. They hold back the waves and unleashed the power curves. The most powerful force on Mother Earth. The WATERS!! Looking towards the threshold of the Great Square a purple haze consumed the core of the four corner stones stars. Your could hear the roaring and pounding of many horse hooves, the blue lighting struck and the four corner river stones exploded in to fireworks. A sonic boom hit the seventh heavens it raddled all souls. Sparks flew, the coachmen came bursting forth though the great square with flying colors. Turning the heavens aqua marine snowflakes, each flake carrying its own special code, which when hit the temple floor became the sea salts and the flavor of Mother Earth, her sea salt soul companion. "The Sea Galley sister's. The rumbling and roaring of the turbulent unsettled seas, the untamable mystical magical oceans seven of mother earth! Whole lot of shaking going on.

As soon as the sea salt was hove deep the coachmen commanded; Wow" hold your horses!" Wow, wow all came to roaring halt, the mustangs full of cosmic earth, wind, fire and cosmic energy's, having little control of their spirits, ready to run the race, and take the heat.

"THE BLACK LIGHT MUSTANGS" A HOLY ROLLING TEAM.

The coachmen were gifted twenty-one thru breed majestic powerful spirits the age of reason. The six coachmen horses the couples of mongolism, relationships, and team work, equality, the love makers and family, the age of family and team work. The nine simpletons, the Clydesdales the roc solid power houses of stability. This team of thirty-six horses adds up to the number of humanity. All heads restless, tossing and raring and ready to go man go!!!! The three Mothers held the waters back, fully impregnated ready to gush fourth their holy force. The most powerful force on Mother /Earth "Birth". Watch this power house unfold!

The coachmen must hold back the forces, until the command is barked. The roar of the powers grew louder with every heart beat, hip hoping, head swing, stirring up the conquest to let Wind Rivers run! They must hold back until the Graces are handed down, and the clock gongs twelve times from north wind, the trumpet sounds from east, and seven hoots from west. A whistle from the south... And the gathering of elders and master minds "The magical mid-night hour" The holy of holies.

Heart throbbing, moment! The Phoenix Says SILINCE Silence filled the heavens with only the tinkering of Florence's tiny wind chimes, and the heart beats of all and the roaring of the oceans. You could feel the power. Then the Phoenix told the coachmen, well done my pet well done! the Coachmen bowed with a rolling, pleasing deep bark Saying THANKYOU –THANKYOU VERY MUCH as Elves would say, Know lets finish up the old so we can move onto the new.

INDIGO TEMPLE

The Phoenix instructed the six couple to go to Mercy's temple take Florence's cosmic yellow tail ribbons. Each couple holding an end and tie them around the vistas. Coachmen you book with me to Indigo's Temple. Mercy was still holding Indigo in her wings with kit gloves, as the rest of her life was being washed away by her own blue blood.

The Phoenix and the Coachmen appear, Mercy lays her down in front of her temple. The Phoenix asks for the Indigo feather weight sphere, placing it on her chest. The other twelve elders gathered around her to say the Holy nine words together. They all touched her clapping to the left then, raised their wings above, as they clapped each word, then finished the last claps to the right, all touching her again. The smoke began to rise with the scent of myrrh and Franken scent at that moment the Phoenix neon blue lighting, struck the temple the thunder rolled. Her temple was re-ignited and the flame restored turning everything Indigo blue. Indigo was taken back to Mercy's temple where the others were for the final count down.

The Phoenix and all the elders gathered, in the sacred grove. Tying a yellow ribbon around the old oak tree until it was finished. Asking the coachmen, have you the spheres, orbs and the colored ribbons to get this ball rolling? I DO with a deep rolling bark, proud to carry them!!! Take the seven seed souls to Graces Temple. She is pure in heart and she will keep them safe with faith until we are called once again.

BANQUET OF GRACES

The Coachmen took top honors at the banquet of graces setting next to the Phoenix. Then all the elders, honored guest speakers, and maidens of faith lined the tables. Then thousands of others trail gazers lined the palace walls, court yards and golden green pastures. All were served Fruit of the vine, Milk for the babes and meat for the aged. The Phoenix snapped his wing, blue lighting rolled from the tips of his wing. His power curve struck the strobe light it began turning clockwise. Let the party begin!

Sticks the announcer, welcome to the party of the sun. This is a rare opportunity to be a part of our own history. We will award tonight all the talents, virtues, gem stones, stars and strips will be gifted, and granted. Names will be changed, to protect the innocent. This special evening has words of wisdom from the elders lend an ear and listen well. Standing ovation, woo hooting, wing clapping, whistling, kaboom broke the sound barrier, rattling all souls. Hearts throbbing, the rhythm of the evening. AAAauuummm filled the palace halls.

The spot light was put one of the Baker Brothers. Sticks speak for the brothers. We are the brothers of substance; we will play an important roll in the ball game of matter on the terrestrial level of mother earth. We will become oracles to which our kindred spirit will speak through draw knowledge, prophecies, insight, thrill seeking stories, fables, and dream, rhymes and riddles. We will house oracles bodies, and cloth the spirits. We are proud to be a part of the whole! Next batter up.

The lights went out, with just the strobe light turning, a new deep vibration sent warmth to all that could fell her like that of the gizmo, rammm filled the crystal palace with everyone joining in, felling the new warmth. Heavenly scent, of evening prim rose rippled from her crystal body. The Curtin of concealment came off. The table was decked around this beauty of wonder, awe filled the palace Rrrraaammm rrraaammm; she vibrated the colors of the rainbow, like that of a firefly. To my fine feathered friends I present to you "THE IRON BUTTERFLY" THE FULLIFMENT OF ONE-HUNDERD –PERCENT- FAITH –AND –NO- DOUGHT! The first gift granted to Diana On behalf of the four faithful vistas yellow, green, sky-blue, and indigo. Standing ovation sonic boom!-

Sticks says, my we proudly present, Diana, from the galaxy of many moons she will become the moon goddess of 'The Blue Beauty' 'Blue moons' and moon Dogs.

"Good last evening to you, I am the true mother of pearls, the huntress of intuitive powers and the reign keeper of the dark side of the moon, and soul sister to mother earth. The ruler of yin and yang ebb and flow, waxing and weaning I am the mother of a thousand breast. Tonight I will share with you one of the great mysteries!" Her soft white and black pearl top hat draped down the center of her forehead with a tear drop amethyst, it flowed across her shoulders and down her back with a soft white halo around her.

She will hold the crown of glory on the blue planet. She will be known by the elders as (Yu) The Master of the arts of the four solar winds and the lunar waters. She will become idolized, as "one who rides the "Blue moon dragon" named Cleo the red, white and blue dragon of let freedom ring! Red mane for blood shed, white tail for surrender, and a blue body for victories and white stars of the redeemed. The great horned owl is her flying companion and comrade named Moses father time. With all dew respect, my I proudly present; The Moon goddess Diana, and her blue dragon, Cleo, the palace roared to be in the presents of such a Master.

I am the huntress of the White Tiger; Fugi and the Black panther; Fang. Once a year when Dog Days swing around Fuji prowls at her door step, of the Great Square in search of his captured lover Fang. With his red eyes of fire, the window to the soul, hepatizing those that gaze upon them. Singing its poetic chants 'come to me!'

The White Tiger is the ray fleer, he comes to devour light, mind, body and soul, nick-named "Worm Wood", he comes from the dark side of the moon. If this devil penetrates the four cornerstones of the Iron Butterflies temples it will be the end my friends, called extinction or belly of the beast. It put a queasy feeling in every one's craws. His target the ring of fire, it will be a place known as the Pacific ring of fire, in search of his lost lover. She rides her red dragon with her archers, the bow and arrows of broken hearts in search of the beast, His preying eyes glowing red with fire, awaits the window of opportunity, as he lurks the cosmos! All the birds feathers stood up on their backs, cats being the most feared. Now I would like to share some insights.

THE CIRCLE OF LIFE

Every sign has its own special perfection. Just as every season of our new years will have its own perfect place. Each sign, each, season, has its own teachings, its own strengths its own perfection. The seasons and signs will integrate, a part of the whole, magical cycles. The cycle of the year the cycle of life all a part of the MANDALA...part of the medicine wheel that is us!! A key to the mysteries, the end of all wisdom is LOVE. A NEW LAW I GIVE TO YOU ...Love one another as I have loved you The Prophet and teacher (JESUS) Silence filled the halls, with the rhymes of the heart beat and rrrrraaaammm her new vibration. It quenched their souls with warmth.

Thank you Diana Next up to bat is her side kicks Two Moons we are proud to announce that we are yin and yang or chi.The offspring of the Queen of our throne. She's the huntress of love makers, the archer the top of her class. She will take top honors in the evolution of cycles on our new mother earth and this galaxy. . Full glory will be handed up to her by her four corner gemstones, goddess. All holding hands in faith to give way to the next, Diana holding the high tides in her hands the keeper of waxing, waning, actions, motion pictures, mood swings, intuitiveness and the powers of the Blue Moon. She will control all public and private affairs. We come from a species of hind's feet that leap, bound and dance. We are the bouncing balls of her purple celestial moons. The pure white stag, its stamina" The valley of the does" the victor. Standing ovation sonic boom, aaaauuummmm rrraaammm.

Sticks returns, Next up, the Man in the moon so to speak. He's one of a kind, the kindred spirit we all desire. The spot light was put on The Coachmen as he got up to the podium in his tuxedo coat. It was a spectacular sight. The black light mustang's manes glowed their trade mark with their shoestring tickling wind chimes. On to the ever lasting decked table, with the iron butterfly humming her tone, the strobe lights sparkling black diamond. The florescent colors from the black lights mustangs manes. And all the guests wearing their favorite colors; it was an ever lasting rainbow of colors, one hell of a light show. Sonic boom aumm, rammmmm. Standing ovation it lasted several minutes. The Coachmen say, THANK YOU, THANK YOU, Thank YOU VERY MUCH with a warm rolling bark, as Elvis would say. I rolled through the cosmos like greased lighting with my red roller skates on. My inner strengths and instincts alone pulled me like a magnet to my destinations. The Galaxy of Knodia on the planet of Golden mean has made me whole to fulfill my destiny.

I AM WHOLE...

I AM FILLED WITH THE LIGHT...

I AM PERFECT...

THE LIGHT FILLS EVERY CELL OF MY BODY...

THE LIGHT SURGES INTO AND THROUGH MY BLOOD... MAKING IT A FOUNDATION OF LIFE, BRINGING PURITY, VITALITY, YOUTH AND BEAUTY INTO MY BEING...

I AM IN THE INFINITE LIGHT AND THE AND THE INFINITE LIGHT IS IN ME...

I AM SURROUNDED BY THE PURE WHITE LIGHT OF THE CHRIST...

NOTHING BUT GOOD SHALL COME TO ME NOTHING BUT GOD SHALL GO FROM ME...

I GIVE THANKS... I GIVE THANKS... I GIVE THANKS...(unknown).

Silence filled the palace; rhythms of their heart beats blanketed the air and warmed their souls with feelings of love.

A heavenly yellow halo glowed from his shining in beingness; all could fell the warmth from these words of wisdom. The spot light still on the coachmen Sticks hands the microphone over to Grace, she quietly takes the floor. I would like to share a poem by Wind River:

> The Iron Butterflies
> Sweeping dove tails, to serve with love
> The spirit warriors flight and fight
> Eagles eye-profound insight
> The challenge, their- race- their fate
> Dream catchers, nightmares run
>
> Blue lighting strikes,
> His Blue thunder rolls, touching all souls

The wings of thunderbird speak
Mighty voice, the majestic powers

"The Legends" Black Light Mustangs run
Free winged spirits fly, heavens place
E'os daughter of dawn, rising
of the sun, white bears felt
Fillies of appeasement kick
their spirits high
Mares of deliverance, innocence,
desire and fate
Pure adoration, kindred
spirits love is in the air
The seven times seven, hooved
wonder of beauty
The scent, the lure, the leap of
faith hope by their side
Holy bivalents, a cosmic wonder
Adore his beauty queen, passions peak

The scent the lure the leap of
faith, hope by their side
The holy waters, shining
diamond's in the rough
The courage of soul, the challenge of flight
The tail of the peacock, full
glory to the third eye
Broken hearts of gold, fallen soldiers, the
arrows of pain, crying eye of the tiger
Spirits set free, the rose peddle pearls
carry them back to the stream of life

The window to the soul the sapphires
gems, the eye of reason
Banquet of graces, gifts bestowed
The iron butterflies, rock
of ages, hold tight!
Have faith sister have faith
Have Mercy's will Pardon
Grace is on your side
Devils claw, battles bind,
blood thirsty tyrants
Eye of the storm, the claws of fate a wait
The trumpet sounds-triumphant!
The golden harp of peace winged
celestial song sings spirit
Let freedom ring, her wind song sings

By Wind River

Then Grace took the floor, this is another Poem by Wind River

PASSIONS PEAK

Minds eye of remembrance kept
Humble beauty in moments spent
Sparks fly, a star is born, mortal,
immortal, rebirth, the soul
The spirit, the guide, turbulent winds,
the golden eagles, eye of the storm,
Holy Ghost await, Ones fate, ones place
The course is set,
Hearts beat, let rhythm runs
Roaring highs, Passions peak,
the point of no return

Eagles Peak, the summit,
faiths, color skies - blue
The victor's flight, the victors might
The courageous coachmen's open gates
Leap of faith, budding wisdoms
Let freedom ring his wind chimes sing

By Wind River

Sticks well did my feathered friend. Our kingdom come our will be done on Earth as it is in heaven. Give us the grace, that we my be pardoned our imperfections and may we shine though the orbs of darkness. My we draw upon the waters, ride the waves of change, and challenge the unknown. My we illuminate and inspire transmute and stabilize our feelings and emotions to energize and heal the physical and vitalize the bodies to come. May we invoke the love wisdom and power of the higher consciousness to guide us to the right activity in the plan on to the path … may nothing but good shall come to us… and may nothing but good shall go from us, we give thanks we give thanks we give thanks amen.

The lights went out the Iron Butterfly still humming with color; The Phoenix raised it's wings and struck the strobe light. Blue lighting came from it's wing tips; it began turning clock wise as 'The Blue Beauty' will spin. It sent a shock wave through the entire crystal palace, electrifying all with their power. His thunder faded into a new sound wave vibration OOOMMM...

All the seventh heavens began vibrating the new sound; it felt wonderful, even better than the butterfly's vibrations. All the guess began OOOMMM, aauuummmig ramming, it was quite stimulating; this went on for several minutes.

All eyes were on the Phoenix, a holy pink aura shines through her in -beingness with soft white light. The bright spot light was still on the Coachmen. The entire kingdom praises your name tonight your name is the Coachmen Tomorrow The shining Dog Star, in the new northern hemisphere, you will become cosmic wondered, a free flying spirit. Yours is the little dog the Greek wonderer name Procyon. He will be the protector and guardian dog to the iron butterflies, the faithful brother. The cosmic wonderers of the home of the brave and land of the free. He smiles from ear to ear.

On mother earth your kind will become an icon a terrestrial scout, on the terrain of and the fertile mother earth. You foot prints in the sand and the bakers snow will reflect who you truly are" The Dog Star- little dog". Standing ovation ooomm auuumm rammm, yours will become a noble companions. then the GEM STONE GUARDIAN

At this time I would like to give the floor to The Gemstone guardian, The Masters of master. My image is in the likens of human beings, Tonight when the clock strikes twelve, all forms will change some into my likeness and become free cosmic deities. And other not so lucky will fall to the Blue beauty some to be celestial and others terrestrial known as mammals.

He had a cape for concealment until the summit of creation is finished. The sweet smell of mother earth filled the palace. My element will run through the liquid veins of mother earth which, will run stone cold as will as the liquid that run though the veins of man called extinction. I will help humanity to have balance, until his soul spirit runs cold. My gemstones will in time heal the bleeding souls of humanity.

I would like to honor Diana first, he pull out from his cloche a gemstone blue indigo bag, with every gemstone imaginable, a gift from planet Atlantes, the holiest of cities in our galaxy of Knodia. To the Queen we present the pearl Rosetta stone terra, you can well imagine its beauty. Next he pulled out a beautiful six pointed crystal pendulum a tool for ray seekers. She will be the Queen of the 'The Great Square 'the iron butterflies the four corner stone temples. The gate that leads to threshold of ever lasting and the jeweled gems of our time honored Street of dreams.

The coat of many colors weaves our past.

The Law of Love in our universe, is that which places the welfare an the concerns an the feeling for others above self; The Law of love is that close affinity with all forces that we associate with as good the law of Love is that force which denies the forces of evil in the world of Hope.((unknown)

Their gems lost in the seas of ignorance, to be bestowed in things to come. The vistas Red and orange simple will receive dim lit stars, a link to the Little Dipper as sisters of deception, possibly a weak link! They are a part of the whole, so they must still have a place.

CHAINED LADIES

These two vistas lost their virginity when they chose self over the others. These three maiden will be chained together for life, known as the chained Ladies, because of their mother's blood, the silver cord that binds us all. And to Dodora a sunk ship she's going down, down, down to the ring of fire, to the ring of fire, to swim in the sea of ignorance, there is no place in the heavens for tyrants, to her we hand FATE!

The four vistas; the iron butterflies rock of ages with their foundations of solid faith. We will present to them the freed spirits plus the quarters of the moon. To Indigo we give the crescent blue moon a rare privilege, she will become the star sapphire of her own start, the brightest star of the four the Big Dipper she will hold the handle and be the corner stone to the Great Square and she holds top honor to her sisters.

These four rocks of faith, will dance to the rhythms of the majestic polar circle of the constellations. Holding hands firmly around the great square as they square dances to the rhythms of the cycles of the constellations. They will dance with perfect rhythm, perfect flow, not to skip a beat, miss the mark, The planet equilibriums at steak, if e tipped off and the planet could become a lost spirit.

Diana the archer must rise up against, the master of the 'Ring of Fire"

On the flip side the Black Panther Named Fang nicknamed (The Big One) she's a ray fleer. She thrives in her black negative energy zones. If she escapes though the doors of the iron butterflies and releases her negative energies it will destroy the plant with an ice age, either ways all terrestrial, and celestial would parish. Fang hissing, growing and scratching at the doors wanting out of the eight houses. To recapture her freedom, and reunite with Fuji in their house of the rising sun, on the dark side of the moon. . Another legend we will resume later!

Silver gold and past experiences are gifted to Indigo. She was given a head dress made of silver leaves and golden bells, with a tear drop star sapphire that covered her third eye. The Statues of a queen, she receives the North Star and the little dipper the brightest in the midnight skies of the northern hemp here.

Our next maiden of honor Mellow yellow the seeds soul given to this maiden, " ALL SOULS DAY" She's to be the goddess of soul ,a kindred spirit to the sun him self. Her colors will merge with all the others of plant Earth. Her faint shining stars rhyme of the heart beat, necessary, for all life on Mother Earth. The tiger's eye, its ambers fire, sparks the seed soul of desires. The entire world will longs for her riches. To yellow we give half moons and divisions, she will be mercy's partner they will hold the hands of fate and fair. She was gifted the eye of the tiger.

The vista green she will be the goddess of emerald cities, green pasture and the still waters, treasures of a heart of gold. She will hold the hands with mellow yellow as she gives way to the third quarter of the moon. Emotions and growth of character a life force all on its own. Kindred colored spirit of Mother Earth. The guardian handed her a pure emerald global necklace.

Next is the sister of voice and vision, as green hands the reigns to sky blue and the full moon of Diana. To sky blue we give the blue velvet skies of night and the sky blues of day. We give to this sister the dawn of pink Rubellite and the dusk of Blood stone. The daughter of reason, maturity and the age of accountability.

Diana the strong hold of the full moon, she holds the keys of to the constellations, and will control the water of the rainbow falls, and all pouring of emotion... Her life force will influence all on the planet earth. She was handed another gift, a Moon Stone necklace.

Florence; the Mother of pearl on her planet golden means, the deliverance of the Age of Aquarius. She was given a necklace of purple Rainbow fluorite. When our first morning brakes, she will bring the dawning of Aquarius! She will hold the horses and the wake of the colored sea walls of the waters. Ready to pour the rainbow water falls into the sea galley though the four corner river stones. ROCK SOLID, holding back their positions. The Palace roared with a standing ovation, sonic boom OOmm, AAAUUUUMmm, rraaaamm.

Sticks say was not that fabulous Thank you very much for your gifts and great wisdom.

The summit of our evening will be our very own Master Mind the Phoenix he will share the prophecies of the Alpha and Omega. A humble Thanks to Wind River for her outstanding insight. The whirlwind, spirited entity of the light of love. I am will pleased by her totality and purity. they hand the floor over to the Phoenix

THE ANIMALS APPEAL

Condemned, though innocent, to die
We plead for pity- hear our cry
If you yourselves would mercy gain
Spare us the wrong of needless pain
Needless- for in the master plan,
Nature provides food for man
Let not it be misunderstood
Wash and be clean, there
hands are stained
In their Dominion, over us
Know that there is an eye to see
The tale-tell things now hide
nor seek, from sight
Oh! Heed the warning-break away
From cruel customs the
painful baneful way!-
Remember the hands of fate
Brings retribution soon or late
Have mercy, the souls to wait
They'll long to do his holy will
To speed their lagging hearts appeal
There steps behind until apathy fills
there hearts with tearful joy or remorse.
To help the helpless and oppressed

Is the golden rule confined?
In practice only to mankind?
Should terror and dread, and
death come to us instead?
Could you once suffer in my stead?

Then would you still, as now
remain - Indifferent to our pain?
Think not because you hear on voice
Our cries, no listening ears have found
Our is it you close you eyes
Then no ghostly scenes can arise-
Ties the hands that crave our flesh
Another hand my use the knife-
Tis to them we lose our life
Immunity from guilt and shame?
Is there no moment when, when they
will hear, cries of the innocent!
The voice of Adam still holds true,
A voice that whispers in the ear
—to trust in the Golden Rule.
Is Paradise to be regained?
By pouring fuel upon our pain
Of passion and impure desires
They were not formed beasts of prey
Be true to your self- begin today

So in our feeble words we plead
Let Live! Be free we prey
Is cruelty only just a wrong?
When suffered by the great and strong
May the spirit the light in every man.
Reveal to you the perfect plan
Man will hold his power in trust
To be worthy one must be just!
Did not the creator not intend
that you should be my friend?
Awake, and act your destiny's part
Obey the prompting in your heart.

Then they will take their rightful place.
As loved Stewarts of our race
For I mother earth shall give them every seed bearing herb and fruit of the trees, yielding, to them flesh!   (unknown)

The entire palace was silenced by these words (hearts beat, silence fills the air, with mouths dropped open)"Silence speaks"!!!

Our next and final guest speaker is an icon to us all in this moment of time and space everlasting... Welcome **FATHER TIME** wing clapping, whistling, hooting and hollering sonic boom ooommmm filled the palace walls. Om the sound vibration of all creation, carry it with you from tomorrow on and there after, it will sooth your souls, and lift your spirits, is vibration will also sooth the souls of humanity if they are willing to try. Time will become the essences of immortality, use it well!

My kindred spirit the sand man, the deity of dreams, "his trade mark" ,"field of dreams" , the unknown hours of the dream catcher's and quantum's leap. The night mares run, heaven or hell, terror trot's .The seven times seven, the gate way to the mystery's and the street of dreams.!,

Tonight he is at the house of the condemned their final count down. His crystal etched hour glass awaits its turn. He catchers all in his dream catchers web that weave the reality of the subconscious mind, realm of the sand mans... (It's just a matter of time) when all is said and done, take hath" USE YOUR TIME WISEY" and" "LISTEN WELL" He will bear many gifts though the ages. In his fruitful field of dream, and the sands of time.

ALTECO'S DUNGEON

Alceto's trade mark (THE BLACK WHOLES) her fortress, her force will suck you in if to close to her vortex. From which there is on escape the venues fly trap. Eye's wide open burning from the pressure. You can hear the agonies, moaning, groaning, weeping, whelping whaling, grinding of teeth, crying and sobbing all a round you, as they scrape and fall up next to your sensitive body with zero gravity and extreme pressures. Some souls falling faster, some falling slower, some are hot and some are cold and they smell of death, ash and dirt. Part's breaking off as they tough your sinking body, leaving their lost soul foul scent in the air. The living hell of Alceto, Emptiness fills the void of immortal falling souls and total darkness consumes the core of the lost spirit to be devoured by that of the ray fleers eternal.

Her red fire breathing dragons. A gift from Kudaline the serpent goddess of the RING MASTERS and the ring of fire. They came roaring in like red wild fire. You could hear their swirling flames a blaze, and feel their heat. Dodora was shackled to the top of the smoking stagecoach with cut throats pocking and jabbing fun at her, drooling, for the feast at hand. Dodora could feel the heat from the ringmaster, almost unbearable hot, her feathers and toes curled. Singing their motto "damnation, lives! Cutthroats singing 'Kick them when there down".

The Seven condemned now, stretched out to the limit. Time for the birds to walk plank, take the plunge, and sink the boat, ride the waves of the ignorant. These vistas are literally hanging on by the silver cords that bind. (FAITH)! She laughs with the laugh of the devil himself or herself.

Its time to pay the Pied Piper; the boogie man. With his caravan of hot house divisions and sharp doubled edged hot blades. You could hear the blades ring an eerie tune, the swishing, slashing striking sawing and chopping the sound of his song and dance.

His temple the band wagon of anacondas-wolf dragons, body of a most powerful serpent, tail of a jagged dragon, head of a gray wolf, mouth of the great white shark., wings of the falcon. The grim reapers' door keeper of the black holes, the dog eat dog, and the black doves of agony and pain. And his prized pet the black spotted owl that looks like the zenith of mid-night sky. All their eyes glow red like the cougar; the birds from pure hell! Fight or flight, their flocks ready and willing to serve with vengeance! THEBIRDS! from Albert Hickcock!

Mercy told the seven your blood is tainted that runs through your vain; it must become extinguished. You hemispheres must be divided Red coats to the right, which breeds condemnation and blue coats to the left which feed the souls and rules the heart. The blue bloods well fill no pain but the redcoats well fill the agony of defeat. I am the deity of divisions and am finished. CUT LOOSE!! Mercy went to the party of the sun. She vanished.

You're in the claws of Alceto and the Boogie man bird and the iron men of chains. The Pied piper, as he plays his tune on his fiery flute. Let our party begin with her wicked laughter, Bring out the song and dance of the singing wicked divas. Let's finish off these, retched souls. Alceto screeched, fire came from her wicked soul bring out her Ring masters. Hundreds of filthy Mick nastiest surrounded the condemned. There was no other fear seeking kill thrill that compared to this feeding frenzy. Trunks still housed the soul, which was the next act that follows.

The boogie man stoked up his furnace, to the point of liquid fire, bouncing balls of liquid fire, jumped out like popcorn, landing on the redcoat halves with a splat of oozing tar you could hear the sizzling of skin and feathers. Leavening crater scars that oozed black tar from them. Alceto called on her red hot tyrants, let's twist some feathers and roast some hide with her wicked laughter. Let's pluck and twist some quills, to get to the soft sensitive skin. Bare naked skin is the best for torture. As dozens of cute throat move in snipping, jabbing, cutting, kicking, spitting their stinking cat breath on their open wound stinging, every slices. They picked indigo showing no mercy, pecking her all most bone clean. Devouring every inch of the red coats, leaving her heart wide open.

Pied Piper says, to hell with this! When push comes to shove, there mine! BACK OFF, AS HE KICKS CUTETHROATS OUT OF THE WAY, Mercy gave me the power for the final blow. I am the butcher of doubled edged sword of divisions, Father of Alcteo and brother to Mercy. born for the wrath of the fallen souls..

Cut loose the vistas so that we can work them over. Dodora and her favored to the right of me and the other four to the left. First he takes Indigo, smudges what's left of her with ash between her foreheads, in tongs he speaks his own sacred words then brings up the branding iron from behind him, marks her forehead, he revs up his power tools puts his cutting edge to the test then does the deed. As he speaks in red hot tongs. To the right fell a pile of true blue ashes, to the left a fell a freed spirit? Indigo freed spirit fell on to a pile of FEATHER into the wings of Grace saying to her will done sister well done, The three faithful sisters Yellow, Green and Sky Blue saw the same fate, smuggled, branded and divided. Their pure colors fall the same way.

Red and Orange where shaking in their boots, scared to death of the wrath that awaits them. Red was the bold one, and said to her mother, you're the one that has brought this on us. We trusted your wisdoms and you let us down, we were once pure in heart like our sisters, but now we are condemned. May you your karma repay you for the damage done, and your soul live in burning hell!

Get the feathers out, Lets tar and feather these three remaining reached souls, they were smuggled, and branded.

<<<<the Pied Piper, started blowing his flute, the fat lady sings her tune along with the cut throats. The birds of vengeance, Grim reapers Jaws, tyrants of war the dragons, and the other a dancing, singing demons joining in on the band wagon. It was

horrifying music. The black doves of disheartenment descended on her, singing the song of "lonesome souls".

We will put a curse on Dodora and her six daughter gravity will be the death of her, and the first to take the breath of life, but it will be betwixt her reach, The cravings of her empty womb, never to be satisfied, the longings of the flesh will consume, her to the point of insanity. She will devour all who trod upon in her path. She will be gated by the "ring of fire". Her tyrant Kundlini she will rule her mortality and her carnival mind. She will live thousands of years in a mortal body, in the vast wilderness of the abyss. Ignorance is her atrocity and she will be known as the black pearl of deception, She will be tormented by the elements, crave the flesh of desires and be weigh down by the me- mine-and-I, ways of the ignorant!

She will hear but not understand; she will see, but only from a distance she will smell but faint, her torment the scratching of the sands of time. Her body will not tolerate the fire bird; she will become a ray fleer. The Pied Piper heated up his blades until they where orange glowing hot, they vibrated there own tone from the liquid furnace. I am the grim reaper the saw blades of divisions "may your hell freeze over" as he bring the axe down, severing the two halves. Her ashes turned into sea salt and black sand she and hers where swooped up by the sand man and the four winds consumed them. Tongora will be your new name in living hell start paddling! Sucking them down Deception pass back into the field of dreams, as she pearl dive out of the heavens. THE END ... Let freedom ring, may your heart string sing ,may the light of Wind river move your spirit!

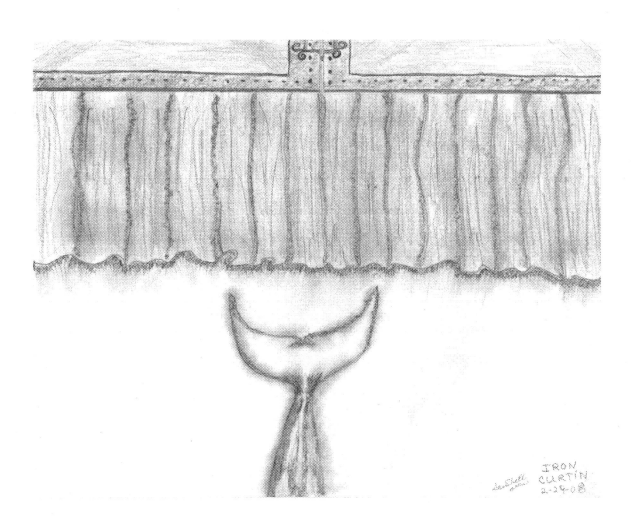

THE ANIMALS' APPEAL

Condemned, though innocent, to die-
I plead for pity- hear my cry-
If you yourselves would mercy gain
Spare me the wrong of needless pain.
Needless- for in his Making's plan.
Nature provides the food for man-
Is there no moment when you hear
The voice to Adam still holds true,
A voice that whispers in your ear:-
to Trust in the Golden Rule!!!
 Let it not be misunderstood.
"Wash and be clean- -
your hands are stained

In your Dominion over me
is Paradise to be regained
Know that there is an Eye to see
by pouring fuel on the fire
The tell-tale things now hid from sight-
Of passion and impure desires?
The darkest spot shall see the light.
You were not formed a breast of prey
Oh! Heed the warning- break away
be your true Self- begin to-day.
From cruel custom's the
painful baneful sway-
Remember that the hand of fate
Brings retribution soon or late.
So in my feeble words I plead
Let us at least be free one day
Is cruelty only just a wrong
When suffered by the great and strong
My Spirit the light in every man
Reveal to you thee perfect

PLAN

You'll long to do His Holy will.
To speed your lagging steps,
steps behind, until
And is the Golden Rule confined
my apathy fill your heart with
tears of joy or remorse,
In practice only to humankind?
To help the helpless and apprised.
Death comes to me with terror dread-
Could you once suffer in my stead
Man only holds his power in trust
Then would you still, as now, remain
and to be worthy must be just.
Indifferent to all my pain?
Did the Creator not intend

Think not because you hear no sound
that you should be my guiding friend?
My cries no listening ear have found,
Or that because you close your eyes
Awaken and act your destined part-
No ghostly schemes can then arises-
Obey the promptings of you heart-
Another hand my use the knife
Then will you take your rightful place
But 'tis for you I lose my life-
As loved protector of our race.
Craving my flesh, how can you claim
"for I give you every herb bearing
Seed and the fruit of the tree
Immunity from guilt and shame?
Yielding seed, to you it shall be for **meat!**
MEAT."

I AM WHOLE

I am whole
I am filled with the light...
I am perfect
The light fills every cell of my body
The light surges into and
through my blood...
Making it a foundation of Life,
bringing Purity, vitality, youth
and beauty into my being...
I am in the infinite light and
the infinite light is in me...
I am surrounded by the pure
white light spirit...
Nothing but good shall come from me
nothing but good shall go from me...
I GIVE THANKS I GIVE THANKS
I GIVE THANKS...

THE LAW OF LOVE

The law of love is that which places
the welfare an concerns an the
feelings for others above self;
The laws of love are that close affinity with
all forces that we associate with good;
The law of love is that force which
denies the wickedness in the world

THR CIRCLE OF LIFE

Every sign has its own special perfection.
Just as every season of the year
has its own perfect place.
Each sign, each, has its own teachings;
own strengths its own perfections.
The season, and sign, are all integrated
a part of the whole, magical cycle...
The cycle of the year, the cycle of life...
There each a part of the (MANDALA)...
part of the medicine Wheel...that is us...
The key to the mysteries Venus the power
of love the end of all wisdom is LOVE LOVE
The law I give to you;
Love one another as I have loved you!!!
                        Wind River

THE IRON BUTTERFLIES

Sweeping dove tails, to serve with love
The spirit warriors flight and fight
Eagles eye-profound insight
The challenge, their-race-their fate
Dream catchers, nightmares run

Blue lighting strikes,
 His Blue thunder rolls, touching all souls
 The wings of thunderbird speak
Might voice, the majestic powers

"The Legends" black light mustangs run
Free winged spirits fly, heavens place
E'os daughter of dawn, rising
of the sun, white bears felt
Fillies of appeasement kick
their spirits high
Mares of deliverance, innocents,
desire and fate
Pure adoration, kindred
spirits love is in the air
The seven times seven, hoofed
wonder of beauty
The scent, the lure, the leap of
faith hope by their side
Holy bivalents, a cosmic wonder
Adore his beauty queen, passions peak

The scent the lure the leap of
faith, hope by their side
The holy waters, shining
diamond's in the rough
The courage of soul, the challenge of flight

The tail of the peacock, full
glory to the third eye
Broken hearts of gold, fallen soldiers, the
arrows of pain, crying eye of the tiger
Spirits set free, the rose peddle pearls
carry them back to the stream of life

The window to the soul the sapphires
gems, the eye of reason
Banquet of graces, gifts bestowed
The iron butterflies, rock
of ages, hold tight!
Have faith sister have faith
Have Mercy's will Pardon
Grace is on your side
Devils claw, battles bind,
blood thirsty tyrants
Eye of the storm, the claws of fate a wait
The trumpet sounds-triumphant!
The golden harp of peace winged
celestial song sings spirit
Let freedom ring, her wind song sings
                    By Wind River

PASSIONS PEAK

Minds eye of remembrance kept
Humble beauty in moments spent
Sparks fly, a star is born, mortal,
immortal, rebirth, the soul
The spirit, the guide, turbulent winds,
the golden eagles, eye of the storm,
Holy Ghost await, Ones fate, ones place
The course is set,
Hearts beat, let rhythm runs
Roaring highs, Passions peak,
the point of no return
Eagles Peak, the summit,
faiths, color skies - blue
The victor's flight, the victors might
The courageous coachmen's open gates
Leap of faith, budding wisdoms
Let freedom ring his wind chimes sing
                                By Wind River

THIRD BOOK
TONGORA'S FALL FROM GRACE
TONGORA:

Alpine Cedar,

Kindred spirits, harmonies abode, into a deep mystical forest, called the Pacific Northwest Rainforest. Lend an ear, as this fictional mystical historical happening unfolds.

Our mediator, Dodona, is the heart, mind and soul of our mystical story. A Satyr (A God of the wood spirit of divinity well seasoned to carry the mother load of this pioneer adventure). With the armor of ancient knowledge and wisdom handed down by her big daddy, Skookum, an ancient Oak which resides with the beech and the redwood cedars ages up to 6000 years in the old growth forest of the Sierra desert in California? These well-seasoned oracles have berried within their roots, the hidden treasures that which will sustain our story! (Manley P Hall) The Secret Teaching of All Ages-The "talking trees stood together, forming a sacred grove. When the priests desired answers to important questions, after careful and solemn purifications they retired to the grove. The then accosted the trees, beseeching a reply from the God who dwelt therein. When they had stated their questions, the trees spoke with the voices of human beings, revealing the desired information. Some assert that there was but one tree which spoke-an Oak or a Beech standing in the very heart of the ancient grove. Because Jupiter was believed to inhabit this tree he was sometimes called (PHEGONEAUS) or the one who lives in a Beech tree. Our trees will be the oracles thought which we will reveal our prophecies and visions and dreams.

The Olympic Gods of the rain forest have shined upon this purebred white cedar. They had set aside a very sacred grove for this tree of knowledge to grow to its fullest potential. In addition we have given our ancient trees the privilege of a voice! This mystical grove sets will above the clouds in a remote area called Hurricane Ridge, which is a mile high in the sky, and located in the heart of the Olympic Rainforest. Our cedar tree can hear the Pacific Ocean, feel the winds of change and see the Rockies to the east. In addition, to the south the mouth of the Columbia River which will gust forth the birthing place of the rest of the ancestors to follow. Dodona has a birds-eye view of the entire Peninsula, which was rich in beauty and rare in species and a fertile eco-system where all inhabitants thrived in their homage. In addition, all animals respected each others' space and worshipped the ground they all walked and flew upon. Mother Earth. Where the sun rises to the east, and the stars are set in motion, the planets aligned, a new era is born the blazing fires of humanity will come roaring in and change their lives forever.

Even the Indians, nomads that came down from the North, would only take what was necessary for living their lives in the untamed wilderness. They believed that if they were to take more than they needed that their Spirit Gods would punish them. They also believed that Mother Earth had a big hand that was in control of all life upon the bones of her body, Earth! The Indians were very concerned about conserving nature's gifts, more so than the white man who followed. The Indians believed that the fish, birds, animals, mountains and streams and rivers and the Skookum aged trees were divine spirits and they could teach valuable lessons about life through their inner attributes sent through examples in their natures.

Our totem animals include a mystical bird the Phoenix our own celestial eagle, a wise great horned owl, twelve white doves of peace and love, three ravens, and twelve Mindanao bleeding heart dove, (Actually only living in the Philippines). The other that will play and important role in our story include the villains. The Killer Whale, three Ravens entities, and Mother Nature. Thunder Bird our earthly name for the mystical Phoenix, being the symbolic celestial ruler of all the birds that inhabit the earth and sky. This bird resembles our American Bald Eagle and when these birds sleep, heads tucked under their wings, they resemble the form of the human heart.

(Manley P. Hall-The Secret Teachings of All Ages) The Phoenix, the body of the bird would be described as having been covered with glossy purple feathers, while its long tail feathers were alternated blue and red. Its' head was white in color and its neck was a circle of golden plumage).

The Phoenix is believed to live up to 500 to 1000 years of age and was believed to sustain its life on pure atmosphere alone. He was respected by the Gods also and entrusted with the seven seals that will set humankind free! He was conceded a legendary bird brought back by to life through the mind's eye of memories kept! Our mountains remember him as being a sacred wind spirit. This bird is one of a kind with only one alive at a time, and it procreates itself. When the time draws near it must die, its instincts alone knew it would come to pass, as "all things become instinct".

In addition, the one who carries the torch thereafter? The American Bald Eagle the next generation to carry the torch of light with his time honored traditions. Our nations own celestial eagle, which will be our symbol of "LIBERTY!" "Let Freedom Ring!"

The mascot in out story, Atumara Chinock, which is Indian for heart, mind, body and soul, the redeeming feathered friend to us all. Also, the mundane Lord over all that have a heart beat.

The Great Horned Owl: named Moses. of the frontier bird scouts of the American pioneers plumage on the west. Moses will be one of our earthly advisors and the eyewitnesses of this adventure.

Our cedar tree, Dodora and all living in the canopy forest have heard stories of this giant bird, which we will call Thunder Bird, the forest story goes something like this. Mother Earth had been preparing for thousand of year for the coming of this new species and the coming of the mystical bird the Phoenix. The entire forest had been told stories passed down by their elders of this bird that would be bringing us to the dawning of Aquarius s. Pangora, our mythic Killer Whale meaning devourer of the ignorance, which is swallowed up by the sea and the abyss. We will change her name to Tongora, an entity in the shape of a Killer Whale and descendant of the legendary sea serpent. She has terrestrial powers that reach across the seven seas; The Pacific Ocean being her main abode. Tongora has a ferocious appetite for those who harbor greed, lust, and self-gratification. Her natural instincts are to kill without ever quenching her thirst. She has no regard for anything but herself. Being thick-skinned and one of the biggest bullies that a whale can be, she will be one of the toughest hearts to penetrate. They prey the ocean over in packs; being wolves of the open sea, lurking in the darkness of the abyss for their victims to devour. Wickedness lives in their nature and they call it animal instincts or human nature. Ignorance Humanities' Atrocity!

SELECTED BIBLIOGRAPHY

Shark Horoscope For Beginners and Professionals by Ursula Lewis
Pendulum Polarity Therapy by Lawrence Crusoe
Zodiac Reference Guide
The Secret Teachings of All Ages by Manley P. Hall
Gifts From Gemstone Guardians by Ginney and Michael Katz
Velch Finches Age of Fables Beauties of Mythologies by Reverend J.
Laugheran
Unknown Authors: I am Whole Confirmation, Animals' Appeal

Chart Your Own Horoscope (Ursula Lewis)
Grossetta Dunlap Publishers New York
Copyright 1976 USA

Bulfinch's Age of Fables of Beauties of Mythology
Philidelphia Rev. J Loughran scott DD
David McKay Publishers
610 South Washington Square
Copyright 1898 by David McKay

Gifts of the Gemstone Guardians (Ginny Katz Michael Katz)
Golden Age Publishing Copyright 1989
PO Box 3217
Gresham Oregon 97030 USA

The Secret Teachings of All Ages (Manley P. Hall)
Published by
The Philosophical Research Society, Inc.
Los Angeles, California 90027
Published by
3910 Los Feliz Boulevard
Los Angeles, CA 90027 Copyright 1977 USA